THE ALL☆ AMERICAN CHINESE COOKBOOK

BY
LUCY CHEE McHALE

AND
JOYCE GOLDBERG

HAMMOND®
INCORPORATED
MAPLEWOOD, NEW JERSEY 07040

Chinese calligraphy by William L. W. Sun

Library of Congress Cataloging in Publication Data

McHale, Lucy Chee.
   The all-American Chinese cookbook.

   Includes index.
   1. Cookery, Chinese. I. Goldberg, Joyce, joint author.
II. Title.
TX 724.5.C5M27   641.5951   80-15767
ISBN 0-8437-3363-2

Printed in the United States of America

PREFACE

I was born in Sian, China, a city located southwest of Peking. My father, Chee Ta Peng, was senior aide and confidant to Generalissimo Chiang Kai-shek. In 1949, when the Communists were about to defeat Chiang's Nationalist government, my father fled with our family of seven to Taiwan.

My parents died when I was still quite young, and I was sent to a girls' boarding school, which served very dull meals. Our family often ate in restaurants during holidays. As a result of this exposure, I became interested in how different foods were prepared. During vacations I stayed with my older sister, who was an excellent cook. I helped her prepare dinners, and gradually I began to create my own recipes. I often invited my schoolmates to feast upon as many as twelve different dishes for a luncheon or dinner.

When I had almost finished college, a family friend sponsored me on a visit to Washington, D.C. I taught Chinese to his ten children, and I occasionally prepared Chinese dishes for the family's dinner parties.

Later, when I moved into my own apartment, I often prepared Chinese dinners for friends. Soon I found myself cooking a full-course dinner for a special boyfriend whose only exposure to Chinese food had been almond cookies. I was greatly relieved when he had several helpings of everything on the menu. Soon after that we were wed!

After I was married, I often tried to create new dishes. My husband's job took us to Omaha, Nebraska, where it was difficult to find authentic Chinese ingredients. Chinese cooking, however, was becoming very popular, and I was getting more and more requests to cook Chinese foods for friends. I soon realized how much I would have to improvise because of the lack of "proper" ingredients. I started to adapt my techniques to the American kitchen and to find substitutes for Chinese ingredients.

I spent many hours in the kitchen experimenting with various methods in order to create Chinese meals using substitute ingredients and simplified techniques. Much to my delight, I found that it is possible to duplicate the flavors and textures of authentic Chinese cooking. Friends asked for recipes, and I often held informal classes to teach them my own special preparations.

In San Francisco, where I now live, I often go to Chinatown or to a local Chinese restaurant to dine, then return home and recreate the same dishes using my own methods and ingredients. I could buy the traditional ingredients, of course, but I find it's much easier — and just as delicious — to prepare Chinese foods using streamlined American methods and ingredients from neighborhood supermarkets. Also, instead of following recipes in traditional cookbooks, I try to create original dishes.

Before I met Joyce Goldberg, I had never compiled any of my recipes. After sharing many meals and experiences together, Joyce and I decided to test, taste, work, and rework these recipes so that other people could learn how easy it is to prepare delicious Chinese food in their own kitchens.

Lucy Chee McHale

麥祁矗茜

CONTENTS

· INTRODUCTION

You don't need bean curd, shark's fin, or even 1,000-year-old eggs, to cook the Chinese food in this cookbook. All you need is a little time (not more, however, than for any other type of food), a few utensils, and a few basic ingredients from the supermarket. You'll end up with as good a meal as if you had used all the traditional Chinese utensils, ingredients, and methods. Think of preparing Sweet and Sour Pork, Creamy Chicken Corn Soup, or Stir-Fry Fish with Vegetables as simple, everyday meals without the elaborate preparation and time-consuming methods found in more complicated Chinese cookbooks!

Here, sauces and marinades are prepared in advance and then combined with the main ingredients according to the particular recipe. Cutting and slicing can be done ahead of time for any recipe. Just remember that *all cut foods must be tightly covered and refrigerated until ready to use.* This preserves vital nutrients that can be lost when cut foods are exposed to air.

You can use this cookbook to serve meals either "American" style or Chinese style. In a traditional Chinese meal, each person eats a little bit of each dish rather than a large portion of one food. A Chinese dinner for four from this cookbook might include Hot Sour Soup (a spicy beginning), followed by Almond Chicken, Beef with Broccoli, and Stir-Fry Scallops, and accompanied by a bowl of steaming rice.

A properly planned Chinese-style dinner includes at least one poultry, one meat, and one fish dish—complemented by appropriate vegetables. Spicy foods should be balanced with those that are more bland, and crispness should be contrasted with some soft-textured foods. As you become more accustomed to cooking Chinese foods you will see how some dishes (such as soups) can be totally prepared in advance, then kept warm in their pots to free you for last-minute stir-frying required in some other dishes.

You can also use this book as you would any other cookbook — for a main dish, accompaniment, dessert, etc., and fill in whatever else you would like. For example, a simple meal of hamburgers can be superbly accented by Chinese-style Potato Salad. Or you might select a main dish of "Lion's Head" Meatballs and Cabbage, and complement it with mashed potatoes and a light dessert. Cornish Hens with Savory Rice Stuffing needs only a green salad to make it a complete meal.

Chinese-style dishes blend meats and vegetables in ways that coax more flavor from both, so you don't have to buy large amounts of expensive cuts of meat. Round steak is most commonly used for beef dishes, although your butcher might suggest another cut that is more popular in your locality.

Many soups can be meals in themselves. Home-style Egg Noodle and Chicken Soup calls for only one chicken breast, yet can serve as a nourishing light meal for at least four persons because of the nutritious combination of protein, vegetables, and starch.

Almost all seafood dishes include vegetables, and some vegetable dishes brim with seafood. Stuffed Tomatoes with Chicken and Shrimp is an exciting yet economical combination of flavors and textures.

Vegetables and chicken are combined in numerous ways. Curried Chicken with its use of potatoes is delicious and hearty. Meatballs with Spinach and Chinese-style Beef Stew are only two examples of tasty ways of preparing inexpensive meats.

Sweets and desserts are not often served in Chinese-style meals. The meals usually end with fresh fruit. We have included a few simple dessert recipes here, however, to complement your meals.

The recipes in this book make it possible to cook Chinese dishes any day of the week rather than saving their preparation for special occasions only. They provide many distinctive flavors with only a few basic ingredients.

So when you ask yourself, "What should I make for dinner tonight?" — Think Chinese . . . the easy way!

Essentials of
Simple Chinese Cooking

You'll need a few utensils to follow the recipes in this book. First, make sure you have a large covered fry pan or a wok. A wok is more efficient for Chinese cooking because it provides better concentration of heat and a smaller surface for the cooking oil to cover, but a fry pan can be used successfully. You'll also need a sharp, fairly heavy knife such as a chef's knife or cleaver, a long-handled spoon for stirring, and a wide metal spatula for lifting and turning foods.

Onions, soy sauce, cooking sherry, sesame oil, garlic powder, ginger powder, white vinegar, vegetable oil, salt, black pepper, sugar, and cornstarch should be considered staples. Soy sauce varies in taste according to whether it's light, medium, or dark. We used a dark soy sauce (which is the one usually found in supermarkets) for our recipes. Frequent use is made of flour, baking soda, chicken bouillon, ketchup, and fresh gingerroot.

Cutting and slicing may seem time-consuming at first but will become easier after you get used to your knife and to the different kinds of cuts. It's best to do as much slicing as possible in advance of cooking a particular dish. Then tightly wrap the cut foods and refrigerate them until ready to use.

Beef is much easier to slice when it is frozen until firm. The grain of the meat is easy to see, and you can get nice, thin slices. The slices are then usually cut into small pieces and marinated, which helps to tenderize the meat. You can do all of this in advance and cover and refrigerate the marinated meat until you are ready to cook.

Chicken and pork can also be sliced or cubed easily when frozen until firm.

Vegetables are sometimes cut diagonally. Diagonal slicing is accomplished by tilting your knife away from you at a 45° angle to the food. To chop an onion, cut it first from top to bottom. Place the cut side down on your chopping board and cut through the onion vertically, then horizontally.

Specific instructions for slicing other vegetables are given in the appropriate recipes.

Always associate the word *stir* with *cook*. Constant stirring is necessary to blend all the ingredients well and to distribute the heat evenly. Chinese cooking is done over high heat, and you should therefore use a quick-stirring motion. Quick-stirring also prevents the food from absorbing too much oil. The high heat, quick-stirring method preserves the vitamins and minerals in meats and vegetables.

All of the recipes in this book were tested on an electric range and timed with a stopwatch. You might have to adjust your range temperature slightly higher or lower. Be careful not to use too high a temperature, or the food will burn. Use your own judgment in cooking, and adjust times and temperatures accordingly to produce excellent results.

HORS D'OEUVRES

熱盆

If you want your dinner, don't offend the cook.

CHINESE PROVERB

NOTES

FILLED BISCUIT HORS D'OEUVRES

An easy version of delicious Chinese steamed buns

Preparation time: 45 minutes
Cooking time: 15 minutes

Makes 40 buns

- **1 pound lean ground beef**
- **3 tablespoons chopped onion**
- **1 egg**
- **1 teaspoon salt**
- **1 teaspoon sugar**
- **3 tablespoons soy sauce**
- **1 tablespoon sesame oil**
- **½ teaspoon ginger powder**
- **1 package (10-12 ounces) frozen chopped spinach, thawed**
- **4 packages (10 per package) refrigerated buttermilk biscuits**

PREPARATION:

- Preheat oven to 375° F.
- Mix ground beef with onion, egg, salt, sugar, soy sauce, sesame oil, and ginger powder. ☐ Drain spinach well, add to meat mixture and blend thoroughly with a fork.
- Separate biscuits. Flatten and thin each with fingertips. ☐ Put 1 tablespoon of filling in center of each biscuit. Bring sides together to form a half-moon shape and pinch tightly to seal.

TO COOK:

- Place on a greased cookie sheet. Bake 15 minutes or until nicely browned.
- Serve hot.

POT STICKERS

Traditionally served for Chinese New Year celebrations in the northern part of China, these succulent dough-wrapped morsels really do "stick to the pot."

Preparation time: 1½ hours

Cooking time: 20 minutes

Makes 40 pot stickers

DOUGH:

3 cups all-purpose flour

1 cup warm water

FILLING:

1 small head cabbage (about
1 pound)
2 cups water
1 pound lean ground beef
3 tablespoons chopped
onion
1 egg
3 tablespoons soy sauce
1 teaspoon sugar
2 teaspoons sesame oil
1 teaspoon salt
½ teaspoon ginger powder
2 tablespoons vegetable oil
1 cup water

SAUCE FOR DIPPING:

2 tablespoons soy sauce
2 tablespoons vinegar
½ teaspoon sesame oil
2½ -3 drops Tabasco pepper
sauce (if desired)

PREPARATION:

- Put flour in large bowl. □ Add water. Mix with hands and knead as smooth as possible (about 2 to 3 minutes). □ Form into a large ball on a floured board and cover with a damp cloth. Let dough rest for at least 30 minutes. □ Meanwhile, prepare filling and Sauce for Dipping.

- Core cabbage and cut into quarters. □ Put water and cabbage in a deep saucepan. Bring to a boil. □ Lower heat, cover and cook about 8 minutes until tender. □ Remove from heat.
- Rinse cabbage with cold water. Drain well and with hands squeeze as much water from cabbage as possible. □ Chop the cabbage as finely as possible and squeeze again to remove excess water.
- Mix meat with chopped onion, egg, soy sauce, sugar, sesame oil, salt, and ginger powder. □ Add cabbage and mix *well*. □ Set aside until dough is ready.

TO ASSEMBLE:

- Knead the dough for a few seconds on a floured board. (Dough should be soft but not sticky.) □ Divide dough into four equal parts. □ Form each into a long rope. Divide one rope into ten pieces. □ With hands, roll each piece into a ball. Flatten slightly. □ With a rolling pin, roll each into a thin (⅛″) pancake about 4″ in diameter. □ Hold the small pancake in the palm of the hand and put 1 tablespoon filling in the center. Close the sides together and crimp *tightly* with fingers to seal. □ Repeat with remaining three ropes of dough.

TO COOK:

- Preheat oven to low.
- Heat 1 tablespoon of vegetable oil in a large (10″) fry pan over medium-high heat. □ Put ten pot stickers in pan, sealed edge up. Brown the bottoms of the pot stickers for about 1 minute. □ Add 4 tablespoons water. Cover and cook for about 3 minutes. □ Remove cover (water should be almost absorbed) and brown for a few seconds. (Do not turn — only bottoms should be brown.)
- Using a metal spatula, transfer pot stickers to a cookie sheet and keep warm in oven. □ Repeat with remaining pot stickers, adding 1 teaspoon of oil before each batch is put in the pan and 4 tablespoons of water after each batch has browned for a minute.

- Serve hot with Sauce for Dipping.

ONION CAKES

Whole onion cakes can be used instead of potatoes or bread, or they can be cut in small pieces for snacks or hors d'oeuvres.

Preparation time: 45 minutes

Makes 8 pancakes

Cooking time: 24 minutes

> 2 cups all-purpose flour
> 1 cup boiling water
> 2 tablespoons vegetable oil
> ½ cup finely chopped green
>   onion
> 1½ teaspoons salt
> 4 teaspoons vegetable oil

PREPARATION:

■ Put flour in a large bowl. Stir in boiling water with a fork. □ Knead dough until soft and smooth, 2 to 3 minutes. □ Divide dough in half and roll each half into a ball. Flatten one ball with palm of hand on a lightly floured board. □ Roll into a large (12″) thin pancake.

■ Using fingers, spread 1 tablespoon vegetable oil evenly over pancake. □ Sprinkle with ¼ cup green onions and ¾ teaspoon salt. □ Roll up like a jelly roll. □ Cut in half, then in quarters. □ Hold one quarter upright on palm of hand, and with the other hand, press to flatten. □ Roll out to a 4″ circle. Repeat with other pieces, making four pancakes. □ Repeat process with other ball of dough, using the remaining onion, salt, and vegetable oil and making eight pancakes in all.

TO COOK:

■ Preheat oven to low.

■ Heat 2 teaspoons vegetable oil in a large (10″) fry pan over medium-high heat. □ When the oil is hot, place four pancakes in the pan. Fry, turning pancakes several times until both sides are brown and crisp (10 to 12 minutes). □ Transfer to a cookie sheet and keep warm in oven. □ Repeat frying process, using remaining vegetable oil for last four pancakes.

■ Serve hot or warm.

DEEP-FRIED SHRIMP HORS D'OEUVRES

The baking soda and oil in the batter combine to make these hors d'oeuvres especially crisp and light.

Preparation time: 20 minutes
Cooking time: 10 minutes

Makes 12 hors d'oeuvres

SAUCE:
- 4 tablespoons water
- 1 tablespoon soy sauce
- 2 teaspoons vinegar
- 1 teaspoon sesame oil
- 1 tablespoon sugar
- ¼ teaspoon ginger powder
- ¼ teaspoon garlic powder
- ¼ teaspoon salt
- ⅛ teaspoon red (cayenne) pepper

BATTER:
- 1 egg
- 4 tablespoons water
- 1 tablespoon vegetable oil
- 4 tablespoons flour
- 4 tablespoons cornstarch
- ½ teaspoon salt
- ¼ teaspoon baking soda

- 1 pound large shrimp (about 12 pieces), peeled and deveined
- 3 cups vegetable oil (approx.)

PREPARATION:
- Mix sauce ingredients in a small pot. ☐ Bring to a boil. ☐ Remove from heat and set aside.
- Beat egg, mix with batter ingredients and set aside.
- Wash and dry the shrimp with paper towels. ☐ Using a small knife, cut along the top of shrimp (do not cut through) and flatten.

TO COOK:
- Heat vegetable oil in a large, deep fry pan over medium-high heat. ☐ Coat each piece of shrimp with batter and drop in hot oil, cut side down. Deep-fry until golden brown. ☐ Drain on paper towels.

- Arrange shrimp on a serving platter and serve with Sauce for Dipping.

CURRIED SHRIMP DEVILED EGGS

A popular American hors d'oeuvre with a Chinese flavor

Preparation time: 1 hour
Cooking time: 15 minutes

Makes 24 hors d'oeuvres

½ **pound raw medium or small shrimp, peeled and deveined (about 6 ounces of meat)**
12 **large eggs**
½ **teaspoon salt**
4 **tablespoons milk**
2 **tablespoons vegetable oil**
1 **tablespoon curry powder parsley, black olives, or cooked tiny shrimp for garnish**

MARINADE:
1 **tablespoon finely chopped green onion**
1 **tablespoon soy sauce**
1 **tablespoon cooking sherry**
1 **teaspoon sugar**
⅛ **teaspoon ginger powder**
½ **teaspoon salt**
1 **tablespoon water**

■ Wash shrimp and dry with paper towels. □ Chop shrimp into small pieces. □ Chop onion. □ Mix shrimp with marinade ingredients in a small bowl and set aside.

■ Hard-boil eggs, peel and allow to cool.

■ Cut eggs in half lengthwise. Spoon out yolks and put in a large bowl. Put whites on a serving plate, cut side up. Set aside. □ Mash and mix yolks with salt and milk. Set aside.

■ Heat vegetable oil in wok or fry pan over high heat. □ Add curry powder. Brown for just a few seconds. □ Add marinated shrimp. Stir and cook for about 2 minutes. Shrimp should be cooked through. Remove from heat.

■ Transfer shrimp mixture to a blender container or food processor and grind as finely as possible, pushing mixture into blades with a spatula.

■ Add ground shrimp to egg yolks in bowl. Mix and mash well until the mixture becomes a thick paste.

■ Fill each egg white with 1 tablespoon or more of shrimp mixture, packing tightly. □ Garnish with small pieces of parsley leaves or small pieces of black olives or a cooked tiny shrimp.

■ Serve at room temperature.

STEAMED EGG ROLLS

These delicate egg pancakes with a seasoned pork filling may be served as a light prelude to an evening meal or for brunch.

Preparation time: 30 minutes
Cooking time: 20 minutes

Makes about 4 dozen slices

½ **pound lean ground pork**

MARINADE:

1 **egg**
2 **tablespoons finely chopped green onion**
2 **teaspoons soy sauce**
1 **teaspoon sesame oil**
1 **tablespoon cooking sherry**
2 **tablespoons cornstarch**
½ **teaspoon sugar**
½ **teaspoon salt**

1½ **teaspoons vegetable oil**
4 **eggs**

- Mix pork well with marinade ingredients and set aside.
- Heat 1 teaspoon vegetable oil in a 10″ fry pan over medium heat. □ Beat eggs in a measuring cup or bowl with a pouring spout. □ Pour in enough beaten egg to thinly cover bottom of pan. (Pour in the center and then tilt pan to cover bottom — as in making a crepe.) Carefully pour out excess. Cook for a few seconds until set. Turn with a spatula and cook other side a few seconds. □ Turn out on board or counter. Repeat to make two more pancakes. □ Add remaining vegetable oil and cook three more pancakes, making six altogether. *Save leftover egg batter for sealing pancakes.*
- Using index finger, spread 3 tablespoons pork filling evenly over entire pancake. □ Roll tightly. Dip index finger in leftover egg batter and spread on end of pancake to seal. Set aside, sealed side down. □ Repeat with remaining pancakes and filling.
- Using a vegetable steamer or steaming rack in a pan with about 2″ of water, steam the egg rolls, seam side down, over medium-high heat for about 8 minutes. □ Carefully remove rolls to a cutting board to cool.
- When cool enough to handle, slice with a sharp knife into ½″ slices on the diagonal. □ Arrange slices on a bed of romaine lettuce.

- If not served immediately, wrap the egg rolls in foil and heat in 375°F. oven for a few minutes just before serving. The egg rolls should be served warm rather than piping hot.

SWEET AND SOUR MEATBALLS

Especially good for parties, these meatballs can be prepared in advance and frozen until ready to use.

Preparation time: 30 minutes

Cooking time: 20 minutes

Makes about 24 meatballs

1 pound lean ground beef

MARINADE:

1 egg
2 tablespoons finely
  chopped onion
2 tablespoons soy sauce
2 tablespoons cornstarch
¼ teaspoon ginger powder
1 teaspoon sugar

SAUCE:

4 tablespoons sugar
2 tablespoons ketchup
2 tablespoons vinegar
1 teaspoon soy sauce
½ cup water

1 tablespoon vegetable oil
2 cloves garlic, crushed
1½ tablespoons cornstarch
  dissolved in 2 tablespoons
  cold water

PREPARATION:

- Mix ground beef with marinade ingredients in a bowl and set aside. □ Mix sauce ingredients in a small bowl and set aside.

TO COOK:

- Preheat oven to 400°F. □ Using 1 tablespoon meat mixture for each, roll into balls. □ Bake on an ungreased cookie sheet for 15 minutes.
- Meanwhile, in a large saucepan or wok, heat 1 tablespoon vegetable oil over high heat. □ Brown crushed garlic for a few seconds. □ Add sauce. Bring to a boil. □ Discard garlic. Add dissolved cornstarch. Cook and stir until the sauce is thick and clear. □ Add baked meatballs. Gently stir and cook a few seconds.
- Serve hot or warm.

TO FREEZE: Bake the meatballs as directed, cool in a bowl, and then freeze in plastic bags. □ Before serving, thaw meatballs, prepare sauce as directed, and thoroughly heat meatballs in the sauce.

MEAT-FILLED PANCAKES

A very popular family-style dish in northern China

Preparation time: 1 hour   Makes 12 pancakes
Cooking time: 16 minutes

FILLING:

- 2 tablespoons finely chopped onion
- 1 large stalk tender celery
- ½ pound lean ground beef
- 1 egg
- 1 tablespoon soy sauce
- ½ teaspoon salt
- 1 teaspoon sesame oil
- ¼ teaspoon ginger powder
- ¼ teaspoon black pepper

PANCAKES:

- 2 cups all-purpose flour
- 1 cup boiling water

- 2 tablespoons vegetable oil

PREPARATION:

- Finely chop celery and onion. □ Thoroughly mix filling ingredients in a small bowl and set aside.
- Put the flour in a large bowl. □ Add the boiling water. Using a large spoon or fork, mix well with a quick-stirring motion.
- When the dough is cool enough to handle, knead for about 2 minutes until it becomes soft and workable. □ Divide dough into four equal parts. □ Divide each part into three pieces (twelve total). □ Roll each piece into a ball and flatten slightly.
- On a floured board, roll each piece of dough into a thin pancake, 5″ in diameter. □ Fill each with about 2 tablespoons filling. □ Hold a filled pancake in palm of hand. With the other hand, gather the edges of the dough up around the filling by folding in a pleating motion. Twist edges tightly together to seal. Gently press the top of the pancake with the palm of your hand until it is ½″ thick and 2½″ to 3″ in diameter. (Don't press too hard—the filling will fall out.) Repeat with remaining pancakes.

TO COOK:

- Preheat oven to low.
- Heat 1 tablespoon vegetable oil in a 10″ fry pan (with cover) over medium heat. □ When the oil is hot, put six pancakes in pan, top side down. Cover and cook for about 5 minutes. □ Turn pancakes over, cover, and cook 3 minutes longer. Both sides should be nicely browned. □ Remove from pan and keep warm in oven. □ Heat remaining vegetable oil in pan and repeat frying process for remaining pancakes.

- Pancakes can be served whole or cut in quarters. Serve hot or warm.

STUFFED MUSHROOMS

In China, we use a similar filling for the popular black mushrooms.

Preparation time: 45 minutes

Cooking time: 20 minutes

Makes 24 stuffed mushrooms

FILLING:

½ pound medium or small raw shrimp, peeled and deveined (about 6 ounces meat)

10 water chestnuts (about half an 8½-ounce can)

4 ounces lean ground pork

2 tablespoons soy sauce

1 tablespoon chopped green onion

2 tablespoons cooking sherry

1 teaspoon sugar

½ teaspoon salt

---

24 large fresh mushrooms, 1½" to 2" in diameter

2 tablespoons vegetable oil

3 tablespoons water

1 teaspoon soy sauce

½ teaspoon sugar

½ teaspoon sesame oil

1 teaspoon cornstarch, dissolved in 1 tablespoon water

PREPARATION:

- Rinse and dry shrimp with paper towels. □ Chop into small pieces. □ Chop water chestnuts very fine. □ Chop onion.
- Put chopped shrimp, ground pork, chopped onion, soy sauce, cooking sherry, sugar, and salt in a blender or food processor container. □ Blend into a thick paste, stopping motor and pushing mixture into blade with a rubber spatula several times.
- Transfer to a bowl. □ Mix in finely chopped water chestnuts.
- Wash mushrooms and remove stems. □ Fill each mushroom cap with about 1 tablespoon filling. Pack tightly so that top of filling is rounded like a miniature cupcake.

TO COOK:

- Heat vegetable oil in 10" fry pan (not wok) over medium-high heat. □ When the oil is hot, add twelve stuffed mushrooms, filling side down. Brown for just a few seconds. □ Remove and put mushrooms on a plate. Repeat with remaining mushrooms. □ Turn mushrooms over, filling side up.
- Return first twelve mushrooms to pan, filling side up. □ Add water. Lower heat to medium or medium-low. □ Cover and cook slowly for about 8 minutes.
- Transfer mushrooms to a large plate, filling side up, leaving juices in pan. □ Add soy sauce, sugar and sesame oil to the pan. Cook and stir a few seconds. □ Add dissolved cornstarch. Stir well until sauce is clear and slightly thickened. □ Remove from heat and spoon sauce evenly over mushrooms.
- Serve warm.

SOUPS

湯

Don't lift off the lid too soon.

CHINESE PROVERB

NOTES

_____
_____
_____
_____
_____
_____
_____
_____
_____
_____
_____
_____
_____
_____
_____
_____
_____
_____
_____

HOMESTYLE CUCUMBER SOUP

A very light and refreshing soup

Preparation time: 10 minutes
Cooking time: 2 hours 15 minutes

Makes 4 servings

2 medium-size cucumbers
1 pound country-style pork
    ribs (or meaty bone from
    pork loin)
1 quart water
2 teaspoons salt
1 teaspoon sugar
1 tablespoon finely chopped
    green onion
½ teaspoon sesame oil

PREPARATION:

■ Peel cucumbers. Cut in half lengthwise. Scoop out seeds. Slice crosswise in ¼″ slices. □ Trim as much fat as possible from pork.

TO COOK:

■ In a medium-size saucepan with a cover, bring water, pork, and salt to boil over high heat. □ Lower heat and with cover slightly ajar, simmer about 2 hours until the meat is tender and starting to separate from the bone. □ Add cucumbers. Raise heat to medium, and with cover slightly ajar, cook 8 to 10 minutes. □ Remove bone, leaving as much meat as possible in soup. □ Add sugar, green onion, and sesame oil. Stir well.

■ Serve hot.

HOT SOUR SOUP

This tastes just like the hot sour soup in Mandarin restaurants, but using a soup mix makes it very easy to prepare.

Preparation time: 25 minutes
Cooking time: 15 minutes

Makes 4 servings

6 ounces lean pork

MARINADE:
2 teaspoons cornstarch
2 teaspoons soy sauce
½ teaspoon sugar

1 cup thinly sliced fresh mushrooms
1 can (8½ ounces) sliced bamboo shoots
1 quart water
1 package beef flavor mushroom soup mix
⅜ teaspoon white pepper
2 tablespoons vinegar

½ teaspoon salt
1 tablespoon cornstarch dissolved in 3 tablespoons water
1 egg
1 teaspoon sesame oil finely chopped green onion for garnish (if desired)

PREPARATION:

- Remove excess fat from pork and slice against the grain into very thin strips, 1″ long. □ Mix meat well with marinade ingredients and set aside.
- Wash, dry, and thinly slice mushrooms. □ Drain bamboo shoots and slice lengthwise into slivers. Set aside.

TO COOK:

- Combine water and soup mix in a large pot. □ Add sliced mushrooms. Stir over high heat until mixture boils. □ Add pork and bamboo shoots. Stir and bring to second boil. □ Add white pepper, vinegar, and salt. Boil about 1½ minutes. □ Add dissolved cornstarch. Stir until slightly thickened. □ Beat egg and *very slowly* pour into hot soup, stirring constantly for a few seconds. □ Add sesame oil, stir well. □ If desired, garnish each serving with a dash of finely chopped green onion.
- Serve immediately.

CREAMY CORN AND CHICKEN SOUP

A hearty soup served often in restaurants in southern China

Preparation time: 15 minutes
Cooking time: 10 minutes

Makes 4 servings

1 whole chicken breast (6-8 ounces meat)

MARINADE:

1 teaspoon cornstarch
½ teaspoon salt
2 tablespoons water

2 cups water
2 teaspoons (or 2 cubes) chicken bouillon
1 can (1 pound 1 ounce) cream-style corn
2 tablespoons cornstarch dissolved in 3 tablespoons water
1 egg
ham, very finely chopped, for garnish (if desired)

PREPARATION:

■ Skin, bone and chop chicken breasts as finely as possible. □ Combine chicken with marinade ingredients. Mix well and set aside.

TO COOK:

■ Bring water to boil in deep saucepan over high heat. □ Add bouillon. Stir. □ Add chicken, stirring quickly with fork to separate pieces. □ Add creamed corn and bring to second boil. □ While soup is boiling, gradually add dissolved cornstarch, stirring constantly as the soup thickens. □ Beat egg. *Slowly* pour into hot soup while stirring constantly. Remove from heat immediately. □ If desired, sprinkle each serving with very finely chopped ham. (It adds color and makes the dish very attractive.)

■ Serve hot.

CHICKEN AND SPINACH SOUP

A very easy and nutritious soup. Be sure not to overcook the spinach!

Preparation time: 20 minutes   Makes 4 servings
Cooking time: 10 minutes

1 whole chicken breast (6-8 ounces of meat)

MARINADE:
2 teaspoons soy sauce
1 teaspoon cornstarch
½ teaspoon sugar

½ bunch fresh spinach
1 quart water
3 cubes chicken bouillon
1 egg
1 tablespoon finely chopped green onion
¼ teaspoon salt
¼ teaspoon sesame oil
⅛ teaspoon white or black pepper

PREPARATION:

■ Skin and bone chicken breast. Cut in half lengthwise. Remove gristle. Cut in quarters lengthwise. Tilt knife away from you and cut against the grain into very thin 1″ pieces. □ Thoroughly mix marinade ingredients with chicken pieces in a small bowl and set aside.

■ Wash spinach well. Break off ends. Break or cut spinach into 2″ pieces. Put in a bowl and set aside. □ Chop onion and set aside.

TO COOK:

■ Bring water to boil in a medium-sized saucepan over high heat. □ Add bouillon cubes and stir until dissolved. □ Add marinated chicken. Stir well, separating the chicken pieces, until mixture comes to a full boil. □ Add spinach. Stir well. Bring to a boil. □ Beat egg and *slowly* pour into hot soup. Stir gently for just a few seconds. □ Add chopped green onion, salt, sesame oil, and pepper. Stir well. Remove from heat.

■ Serve hot.

CHICKEN RICE SOUP

This popular Cantonese-style soup is traditionally served for breakfast.

Preparation time: 20 minutes

Makes 6 to 8 servings

Cooking time: 1 hour 10 minutes

1 chicken breast (6-8 ounces
 of meat)
MARINADE:
2 tablespoons finely
 chopped green onion
1 tablespoon soy sauce
2 teaspoons cornstarch
1 teaspoon sugar
¼ teaspoon salt
½ teaspoon sesame oil

1 cup round-grain (pearl) rice
2 quarts water
4 cubes chicken bouillon
1 teaspoon salt
1 cup finely shredded lettuce (for garnish)
 black pepper (if desired)

PREPARATION:

■ Skin and bone chicken breast. Cut in half lengthwise. Remove gristle. Cut lengthwise into four strips. Tilt knife away from you and cut against the grain into very thin 1″ pieces. □ Chop onion. □ Thoroughly mix chicken with marinade ingredients in a small bowl and set aside.

TO COOK:

■ Put rice in a large, deep pot and rinse with tap water. Drain well. □ Add the 2 quarts of water. Cover and bring to a boil over high heat. □ Immediately reduce heat to low. □ Add bouillon cubes and salt. Stir well. Cover with lid slightly (1″) ajar and cook over low heat about 45 minutes, stirring occasionally. Make sure the cover stays ajar so the rice will not overflow. □ Add marinated chicken. Stir well. Cook 15 minutes longer over low heat, stirring occasionally. Soup should be thick and creamy. □ Garnish each serving with 1 tablespoon shredded lettuce and a little black pepper if desired.

■ Serve hot.

HOMESTYLE EGG NOODLE AND CHICKEN SOUP

This hearty soup with tender egg noodles is a country-style meal eaten often in northern China during the winter.

Preparation time: 20 minutes
Cooking time: 15 minutes

Makes 6 to 8 servings

1 whole chicken breast (6-8 ounces meat)

MARINADE:
2 tablespoons finely chopped green onion
1 tablespoon soy sauce
2 teaspoons cornstarch
1 teaspoon sugar
1 teaspoon sesame oil
¼ teaspoon salt

BATTER:
1½ cups all-purpose flour
2 eggs
½ cup water
1 teaspoon salt

1½ quarts water
4 cubes chicken bouillon
1 cup frozen peas and carrots, thawed
1 egg
¼ teaspoon black pepper

PREPARATION:

■ Skin and bone chicken breast. Cut in ¼" cubes. □ Chop onion. □ Thoroughly mix chicken cubes with marinade ingredients and set aside.

■ For noodle batter, beat 2 eggs, mix with flour, water and salt. Stir for at least 1 minute until the mixture resembles a thick, smooth paste. Set aside.

TO COOK:

■ Bring water to boil in a large, deep pot over high heat. □ Add bouillon cubes. Stir well. □ Add peas and carrots. Cook and stir about 1 minute. □ Add marinated chicken. Cook and stir a few seconds. □ Bring to a boil.

■ Hold a dinner knife in one hand and the bowl with the noodle batter in the other hand. Tilt bowl toward pot. As the batter starts to pour into the bowl, cut off a 2" piece (¼" thick) with knife. Stir soup with knife. □ Repeat cutting and stirring as quickly as possible until all the batter is used. The soup should continue to boil. □ After all the noodles are in the soup, boil 1 minute, stirring constantly. □ Beat 1 egg and *slowly* pour into boiling soup. Stir well for a few seconds. □ Add black pepper. Mix well. Remove from heat. (Total cooking time after the water boils — 8 to 10 minutes.)

■ Serve hot.

EGG AND TOMATO SOUP

The tomatoes add texture and flavor to this dish, which is similar to Egg Drop Soup.

Preparation time: 10 minutes

Cooking time: 10 minutes

Makes 4 servings

3 large tomatoes
1 tablespoon finely chopped
  green onion
1 quart water
4 cubes chicken bouillon
1 tablespoon cornstarch
  dissolved in 2 tablespoons
  water
2 eggs
⅛ teaspoon black pepper
¼ teaspoon sesame oil (if desired)

PREPARATION:

■ Cut tomatoes into 1″ chunks. □ Chop onion.

TO COOK:

■ Bring water to boil in a deep saucepan over high heat. □ Add chicken bouillon. Stir well. □ Add tomatoes. Cover and bring to a boil. Then, with cover slightly ajar, boil 3 minutes. □ Slowly add dissolved cornstarch. Stir well. □ Beat eggs. □ When soup is slightly thickened, *slowly* pour in beaten eggs, stirring gently for a few seconds. Add green onions, black pepper, and sesame oil. Stir well. Remove from heat.

■ Serve piping hot.

SPECIAL OXTAIL SOUP

When I was a college student in Taichung City, I often rode the train home to Taipei for the holidays. I ate in the dining car, where I tasted oxtail soup for the first time. I experimented and came up with this recipe, which is almost like a stew. It's very hearty and freezes well.

Preparation time: 30 minutes

Makes 8 to 10 servings

Cooking time: 3 hours 35 minutes

> 1 whole oxtail (2½ pounds)
>   or already cut oxtail in a
>   package
> 1 small onion
> 3 quarts water
> 3 tablespoons soy sauce
> 1 tablespoon salt
> 1 tablespoon sugar
> 2 tablespoons cooking
>   sherry
> ½ teaspoon black pepper
> ½ teaspoon ginger powder
> 2 medium carrots
> 2 large stalks celery
> 3 large tomatoes
> ½ medium (or 1 small)
>   cabbage (about 1 pound)

- Trim as much fat from the oxtail as possible. Cut into 2″ chunks at joints if you are using a whole oxtail. Rinse all pieces well. □ Chop onion.
- Bring water and oxtail to boil in a large pot over high heat. Lower heat to medium-low. Cover and cook 1 hour. Stir occasionally. □ Add onion, soy sauce, salt, sugar, cooking sherry, black pepper, and ginger powder. Cover and cook for another hour. Stir occasionally.
- Peel carrots and cut into 1″ chunks. □ Cut celery in half lengthwise, then crosswise into 1″ pieces. □ Cut tomatoes into 1″ chunks. □ Core cabbage and cut into 1″ pieces.
- After oxtail has cooked for the second hour, add carrots, celery, tomatoes, and cabbage. Stir well. Cover and cook 1½ hours longer. Stir occasionally. □ When the meat is almost falling from the bone and the soup has thickened, remove from heat. Let stand, covered, about 15 minutes before serving.
- Serve hot.

BEEF

牛肉

Hurry men at their work, not at their meals.

CHINESE PROVERB

NOTES

BEEF WITH BROCCOLI

A very popular Cantonese dish with American broccoli substituted for Chinese broccoli

Preparation time: 25 minutes   Makes 4 servings
Cooking time: 6 minutes

1 pound lean beef

MARINADE:

2 tablespoons soy sauce
1 tablespoon cooking sherry
1 teaspoon sesame oil
½ teaspoon salt
½ teaspoon sugar
¼ teaspoon ginger powder
   (or 1 teaspoon finely
   chopped ginger root)
1 tablespoon cornstarch

½ pound fresh broccoli
2 tablespoons chopped
   onion
4 tablespoons vegetable oil
2 tablespoons water
½ teaspoon sugar
¼ teaspoon salt

PREPARATION:

- Slice beef against the grain into very thin 1½" pieces.
- Mix beef well with marinade ingredients and set aside.
- Cut broccoli into small florets. Peel tough outer membrane from stems and slice on the diagonal into bite-size pieces. □ Chop onion.

TO COOK:

- Heat vegetable oil in wok or large fry pan over high heat. □ Brown onion for a few seconds. □ Add beef. Cook and stir until the beef is almost cooked through, about 2 minutes. □ Transfer beef to a bowl, leaving liquid, if any, in pan. □ Add water and broccoli to pan. Cook and stir about 30 seconds. □ Add sugar and salt. Cook and stir until the broccoli is tender but still crunchy, about 2 minutes. □ Return beef to pan. Mix with broccoli and cook and stir about 30 seconds longer.

- Serve hot.

MEATBALLS WITH SPINACH

Lightly spiced meatballs are served on a bed of seasoned spinach.

Preparation time: 25 minutes

Cooking time: 15 minutes

Makes 4 servings

1 pound lean ground beef

MARINADE:

1 egg
1 tablespoon soy sauce
1 tablespoon cooking sherry
¼ teaspoon ginger powder
1 tablespoon cornstarch
½ teaspoon salt

1 bunch fresh spinach
6 tablespoons vegetable oil
¼ teaspoon salt
¾ cup water
2 teaspoons soy sauce
1 teaspoon sugar
1 teaspoon sesame oil

2 teaspoons cornstarch dissolved in 2 tablespoons water
1 tablespoon finely chopped parsley or green onion for garnish (if desired)

PREPARATION:

■ Mix meat well with marinade ingredients. □ Roll meat into twenty walnut-size meatballs and set aside.
■ Wash spinach leaves and cut in half.

TO COOK:

■ Preheat oven to low.
■ Heat 2 tablespoons vegetable oil in wok or large fry pan over high heat. □ Drop in spinach. Stir and cook 1½ minutes. □ Add salt. Stir and remove from heat. □ Transfer to a serving plate as a bed for meatballs and keep in a warm oven until meatballs are done.
■ Heat remaining vegetable oil in wok or large fry pan over medium heat. □ Drop meatballs into hot oil. Brown on all sides for a few minutes (meat will not be completely cooked inside). □ Drain almost all oil from the pan, leaving the meatballs. □ Add water, soy sauce, sugar, and sesame oil. Bring to a boil. Cook and stir about 3 minutes. Push meatballs to sides of pan. □ Add dissolved cornstarch to liquid in center. Stir until slightly thickened and mix well with meatballs. □ Arrange meatballs and sauce on bed of spinach. Sprinkle with finely chopped parsley or green onion, if desired.
■ Serve hot.

BEEF AND CELERY

Crisply cooked celery and marinated beef combine to make this dish pleasing in texture as well as in taste.

Preparation time: 30 minutes

Cooking time: 6 minutes

Makes 4 servings

1 pound lean beef

MARINADE:
2 tablespoons soy sauce
1 tablespoon cooking sherry
1 teaspoon sugar
½ teaspoon salt
1 tablespoon cornstarch
¼ tablespoon ginger powder (or 1 teaspoon finely chopped gingerroot)

4 large stalks celery
2 tablespoons thinly sliced onion
4 tablespoons vegetable oil
2 tablespoons water
1 teaspoon sesame oil
½ teaspoon sugar
¼ teaspoon salt

PREPARATION:
- Cut beef against the grain into small pieces and then into 1½"-long thin strips.
- Mix beef well with marinade ingredients and set aside.
- Cut celery into 1½"chunks, then slice into thin, lengthwise strips. Set aside. □ Thinly slice onion.

TO COOK:
- Heat vegetable oil in wok or large fry pan over high heat. □ Brown onion for a few seconds. □ Add beef. Cook and stir constantly, separating the beef strips until they change color and are almost cooked through, about 2 minutes. □ Transfer beef to a bowl, leaving liquid, if any, in the pan. □ Add water and celery to pan. Cook and stir 1 minute. □ Add sesame oil, sugar, and salt. Cook and stir about 30 seconds until the liquid is almost absorbed and the celery is crisp and tender. □ Return beef to the pan. Mix all ingredients well and cook and stir a few seconds longer.
- Serve immediately.

CHINESE-STYLE BEEF STEW

A popular American dish with a Chinese twist

Preparation time: 15 minutes
Cooking time: 1 hour

Makes 4 to 6 servings

- **2 pounds beef for stew**
- **3 tablespoons chopped onion**
- **2 tablespoons vegetable oil**
- **2 tablespoons cooking sherry**
- **2 cups water**
- **4 tablespoons soy sauce**
- **2 teaspoons sugar**
- **½ teaspoon salt**
- **½ teaspoon ginger powder**
- **2 large carrots**
- **2 large potatoes**

■ Cut beef into 1½" chunks. □ Chop onion.

■ In a large pot with a cover, heat vegetable oil over medium-high heat. □ Brown onion for a few seconds. □ Add beef. Brown for a few seconds. □ Add cooking sherry and continue browning until the meat changes color. □ Add water, soy sauce, sugar, salt, and ginger powder. Stir well, bring to a boil, then lower heat to low and simmer, covered, about 20 minutes.

■ Peel carrots and potatoes and cut into 1½" chunks.

■ When meat has cooked 20 minutes, add carrots, stir, cover and let simmer about 15 minutes. □ Add potatoes, stir, cover, and let simmer about 20 minutes longer, stirring occasionally until the meat, potatoes, and carrots are tender but not falling apart and the liquid is almost absorbed and thickened.

■ Serve over boiled rice.

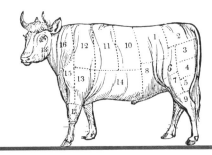

BEEF WITH ONIONS

Its very pungent onion flavor distinguishes this beef dish.

Preparation time: 20 minutes
Cooking time: 5 minutes

Makes 4 servings

1 pound lean beef

MARINADE:

    2 tablespoons soy sauce
    1 tablespoon cooking sherry
    1 teaspoon sugar
    ¼ teaspoon salt
    1 tablespoon cornstarch

    1 large yellow onion
    4 tablespoons vegetable oil

PREPARATION:

- Slice beef against the grain into very thin 1½" pieces.
- Mix beef well with marinade ingredients and set aside.
- Peel onion and cut off ends. Cut in half along the grain, then in half again. Slice thinly against the grain.

TO COOK:

- Heat vegetable oil in wok or large fry pan over high heat. □ Sauté onions for about 1 minute. □ Add beef and mix well with onions. Cook and stir 2 to 3 minutes until the beef is cooked through and the onions are soft.

- Serve hot.

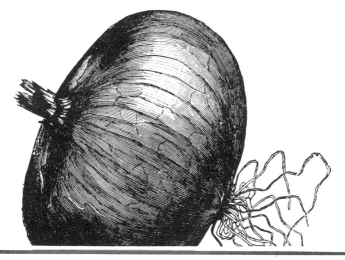

CHINESE-STYLE MEAT LOAF

A traditional American dish turned Chinese

Preparation time: 15 minutes

Makes 4 servings

Cooking time: 1 hour

- **1 pound lean ground beef**
- **2 tablespoons finely chopped green pepper**
- **2 tablespoons finely chopped onion**
- **2 tablespoons finely chopped celery**
- **1 cup cooked rice**
- **1 egg**
- **2 tablespoons cornstarch**
- **2 tablespoons soy sauce**
- **1 teaspoon sugar**
- **½ teaspoon salt**
- **⅛ teaspoon black pepper**
- **¼ teaspoon ginger powder**
- **1 teaspoon sesame oil**

PREPARATION:

■ Combine all ingredients and mix well.

TO COOK:

■ Form into a loaf and bake ½ hour at 325° F. □ Bake another ½ hour at 350° F.

■ Slice and serve hot.

BEEF WITH OYSTER SAUCE

A typical Cantonese dish served often in restaurants

Preparation time: 25 minutes   Makes 4 servings
Cooking time: 5 minutes

1 pound lean beef

MARINADE:
1 tablespoon soy sauce
2 teaspoons cornstarch
1 teaspoon sugar
¼ teaspoon ginger powder

1 medium stalk celery
1 small carrot
2 tablespoons chopped
  onion
3 tablespoons vegetable oil
2 tablespoons water
¼ teaspoon salt
3 tablespoons Easy
  Homestyle Oyster Sauce
  (page 88)
1 teaspoon sesame oil

PREPARATION:
■ Cut beef against the grain into very thin 2″ pieces.
■ Mix beef with marinade ingredients in a small bowl and set aside.
■ Slice celery crosswise into thin slices. □ Peel carrot and slice thinly crosswise. □ Chop onion.

TO COOK:
■ Heat vegetable oil in wok or large fry pan over high heat. □ Brown onion for a few seconds. □ Add beef. Cook and stir about 1½ minutes. □ Transfer to a bowl. □ Add water, celery, carrots, and salt to pan. Cook and stir about 1 minute. □ Put beef back in pan. □ Add oyster sauce and sesame oil. Cook and stir for about 45 seconds longer.

■ Serve immediately.

SPICY SHREDDED BEEF

A very popular Szechuan dish

Preparation time: 35 minutes   Makes 4 servings
Cooking time: 10 minutes

1 pound lean beef

MARINADE:
- **2 tablespoons soy sauce**
- **1 tablespoon cooking sherry**
- **1 teaspoon sugar**
- **¼ teaspoon ginger powder**

- **1 small onion**
- **1 large stalk celery**
- **1 small carrot**
- **2 cloves garlic**
- **3 tablespoons vegetable oil**
  dried red chili peppers (2 or 3)
- **½ teaspoon salt**
- **½ teaspoon sugar**
- **1 teaspoon sesame oil**

PREPARATION:

■ Slice beef in large thin pieces along the grain. Then slice against the grain into thin 1½" strips.

■ Put beef strips in a bowl and add marinade ingredients. Mix well and set aside.

■ Peel onion and cut in half along the grain, then in quarters. Next slice crosswise into thin strips. □ Cut celery into 1½" chunks and slice lengthwise into thin strips. □ Peel carrot, slice crosswise into thin slices. Pile a few pieces together and cut into thin strips. Set aside. □ Peel and crush garlic.

TO COOK:

■ Heat vegetable oil in wok or large fry pan over high heat. □ Add garlic and red peppers. Brown for a few seconds. When the peppers and garlic turn dark and the oil begins to smoke, discard peppers and garlic. □ Add beef. Stir and cook over high heat for 4 to 5 minutes until all juices are *almost* absorbed. □ Add onions, celery, and carrots. Cook and stir for about 3 minutes. □ Add salt, sugar, and sesame oil. Cook and stir about 1 minute until liquid is absorbed. Remove from heat.

■ Serve hot.

PAN-FRIED STEAKS— CHINESE-STYLE

The marinade makes the steaks extremely tasty.

Preparation time: 15 minutes

Marinating time: 2 hours

Cooking time: 10 minutes

Makes 4 servings

**4 pieces (2 pounds)
1½"-thick filet mignon (or 4
Porterhouse or T-bone
steaks)**

MARINADE:

**2 cloves garlic
4 tablespoons water
3 tablespoons soy sauce
2 tablespoons cooking
  sherry
1½ teaspoons sugar
½ teaspoon salt
¼ teaspoon black pepper**

2 tablespoons vegetable oil

PREPARATION:

- Cut each piece of filet in half horizontally, but not completely through. When laid flat, each piece will resemble a butterfly. (If using Porterhouse or T-bone steaks, leave whole.) □ Peel and crush garlic.
- Thoroughly mix marinade ingredients in a small bowl. □ Put steaks in a large bowl, pour marinade over them and let stand at room temperature 1 hour. □ Turn over. Marinate 1 hour longer.

TO COOK:

- Preheat oven to low.
- Heat 1 tablespoon vegetable oil in a large (10") fry pan over medium-high heat. □ When the oil is hot, add two steaks. (If you are using filets, lay each piece flat so it keeps its butterfly shape.) Brown each side 2 minutes (medium rare). □ Remove from pan and keep warm in oven. □ Add remaining vegetable oil to pan and fry other two steaks.
- Serve American-style with baked potato or Chinese-style with rice and/or vegetable.

HOT AND SOUR BEEF

A version of Hunan-style beef—very spicy and flavorful

Preparation time: 25 minutes Makes 4 servings
Cooking time: 5 minutes

1 pound lean beef

MARINADE:
- 1 tablespoon soy sauce
- 1 tablespoon cooking sherry
- 1 teaspoon sugar
- 2 teaspoons cornstarch
- 1 tablespoon vegetable oil

SAUCE:
- 1 tablespoon soy sauce
- 1 tablespoon water
- 1½ tablespoons vinegar
- 1 teaspoon salt
- 1 teaspoon cornstarch

- 3 tablespoons vegetable oil
- dried red chili peppers (3 or 4)
- cloves garlic (3 or 4)
- 3 tablespoons chopped onion
- 1½ cups cabbage

PREPARATION:
- Slice beef against the grain into very thin 2″ pieces.
- Mix sliced beef with marinade ingredients in a small bowl and set aside.
- Mix sauce ingredients in a small bowl and set aside.
- Break chili peppers into pieces. ☐ Peel and crush garlic. ☐ Cut cabbage into 1″ pieces. ☐ Chop onion.

TO COOK:
- Heat vegetable oil in a wok or large fry pan over high heat. ☐ Add dried red chili peppers and garlic. Brown for a few seconds. ☐ Add onion. Brown for a few seconds longer. (You may discard garlic and peppers if you wish.) ☐ Add marinated beef. Stir and cook for about 1½ minutes. ☐ Add cabbage. Stir and cook for 1 minute more. ☐ Stir sauce well and add to pan. Cook and stir 30 seconds. Remove from heat. The beef should be tender and the cabbage should be crisp.
- Serve immediately.

PORK

豬
肉

Every family cooking pot has one black spot.

CHINESE PROVERB

NOTES

SWEET AND SOUR PORK

An easy version of an American favorite

Preparation time: 30 minutes   Makes 4 servings
Cooking time: 20 minutes

BATTER:
- ½ cup flour
- ½ cup cornstarch
- 1 teaspoon salt
- 1 egg
- 7 tablespoons water

SAUCE:
- 3 tablespoons sugar
- 2 tablespoons ketchup
- 1½ tablespoons vinegar
- 1 teaspoon soy sauce
- 6 tablespoons water
- 4 tablespoons pineapple juice

- 12 ounces lean boneless pork
- 2 cloves garlic
- 1 small green pepper
- 1 small carrot
- 3 cups vegetable oil (approx.)

- 1 tablespoon cornstarch dissolved in 2 tablespoons water
- ½ cup canned pineapple chunks (reserve juice)

PREPARATION:

- Beat egg, mix batter ingredients and set aside. □ Mix sauce ingredients in small bowl and set aside.
- Cut pork into 1″ cubes. □ Peel and crush garlic. □ Remove and discard seeds and stem from green pepper. Cut pepper into 1″ squares. □ Peel carrot and cut crosswise into thin slices.

TO COOK:

- Preheat oven to 400°F. □ Heat the vegetable oil in a wok or large fry pan over high heat. □ While the oil is heating, add all pork to batter, coating each piece well. □ Deep-fry a few pieces at a time until brown. □ Transfer to pan or cookie sheet and keep hot in oven. (Pork will continue cooking and will become crisp.)
- Remove all oil from pan. □ Put back 1 tablespoon of the oil and heat over high heat. □ Brown garlic. □ When the oil begins to smoke, add green pepper and carrot slices. Cook and stir about 30 seconds. Discard garlic. □ Add sauce. Bring to boil. □ Add dissolved cornstarch. Stir for a few seconds until the sauce is thick and clear. □ Add pork and pineapple chunks. Mix well.
- Serve hot.

SPICY SHREDDED PORK

This dish is also called "pork that smells like fish" because in the Chinese province of Szechuan, the same spices are traditionally used in cooking fish to disguise its fishy odor.

Preparation time: 35 minutes

Cooking time: 6 minutes

Makes 4 servings

1 pound lean pork

MARINADE:

1 tablespoon soy sauce
2 teaspoons cornstarch
½ teaspoon sugar
1 tablespoon cooking
 sherry

SAUCE:

1 tablespoon soy sauce
1 teaspoon vinegar
1 tablespoon water
1 teaspoon sesame oil
½ teaspoon ginger powder
1 teaspoon cornstarch
½ teaspoon salt
1 teaspoon sugar
¼ teaspoon garlic powder

1 medium green pepper
14 water chestnuts (about
 half an 8½-ounce can)
2 tablespoons chopped
 onion

3 tablespoons vegetable oil
2-3 dried red chili peppers

PREPARATION:

- Cut pork against the grain into very thin strips about 1½" long.
- Combine pork strips with marinade ingredients, mix well and set aside. □ Mix sauce ingredients in a small bowl and set aside.
- Remove seeds and stem from green pepper and discard. Cut pepper in quarters and then in thin strips. □ Cut water chestnuts in half horizontally and then in thin strips.
- Chop onion.

TO COOK:

- Heat vegetable oil in wok or large fry pan over high heat. □ Add dried red chili peppers and stir for a few seconds. When the peppers turn dark, remove and discard. □ Brown onions for a few seconds. □ Add pork. Cook and stir for about 2 minutes, separating pork strips. □ Add green pepper and water chestnuts. Cook and stir about 1 more minute. □ Add sauce, stir well and cook about 45 seconds longer.
- Serve piping hot.

MU SHU PORK

This is a very simple way to cook Mu Shu Pork because you don't have to find any mu shus (black fungus and yellow tiger lily flowers). It can be served just as is or as a filling for Chinese-Style Pancakes.

Preparation time: 30 minutes

Cooking time: 10 minutes

Makes 4 servings

¾ **pound very lean pork**

MARINADE:
1 **tablespoon soy sauce**
1 **tablespoon water (or cooking sherry)**
½ **teaspoon sugar**
2 **teaspoons cornstarch**

2½ **ounce can sliced mushrooms**
2 **tablespoons chopped onion**
2 **cups shredded cabbage**
5 **tablespoons vegetable oil**

4 **eggs**
2 **tablespoons soy sauce**
½ **teaspoon salt**
½ **teaspoon sugar**
1 **teaspoon sesame oil**

PREPARATION:

■ Remove all excess fat from pork. Cut against the grain into thin 1"-long strips.

■ Mix pork with marinade ingredients and set aside.

■ Drain mushrooms. □ Chop onions. □ Shred cabbage.

TO COOK:

■ Heat 2 tablespoons of the vegetable oil in a wok or large fry pan over high heat. □ Beat eggs. When the oil is very hot, pour in the beaten eggs and scramble lightly until firm. □ Transfer to a bowl. □ Add 3 more tablespoons oil to pan. □ Add onion and brown for a few seconds. □ Add pork. Cook and stir for about 3 minutes until the meat changes color and is cooked through. □ Add cabbage, mushrooms, and scrambled eggs. Cook and stir about 30 seconds. □ Add soy sauce, salt, sugar, and sesame oil. Cook and stir about 1 more minute. □ For best results, serve immediately, before the dish becomes too juicy. If there is too much liquid, reheat quickly over high heat and add 1 teaspoon cornstarch dissolved in 1 tablespoon water to liquid in center of pan. Stir a few times until the liquid is thickened.

■ Mix all ingredients well and serve hot.

BARBEQUED ROAST PORK

This very popular Cantonese-style roast pork dish is marinated overnight and then oven-roasted.

Preparation time: 15 minutes

Marinating time: 12 to 24 hours

Cooking time: 45 minutes

Makes 4 to 6 servings

>   2 pounds lean pork butt
>   without bone

MARINADE:

>   2 tablespoons water
>   2 tablespoons soy sauce
>   2 tablespoons cooking
>   sherry
>   2 tablespoons ketchup
>   1 tablespoon finely
>   chopped onion
>   2 teaspoons sugar
>   1 teaspoon salt
>   ½ teaspoon ginger powder
>   1 tablespoon sesame oil

SEASONING MIXTURE:

>   1 teaspoon sugar
>   1 teaspoon sesame oil
>   1 tablespoon water

PREPARATION:

- Cut pork into strips approximately 7″ long, 2″ wide, and 1″ thick.
- Thoroughly mix the marinade ingredients in a large bowl. □ Add pork strips and mix well. □ Cover and refrigerate overnight (up to 24 hours). Turn pieces occasionally.

TO COOK:

- Preheat oven to 425°F. □ Line a roasting pan with foil (for easy cleanup). Put meat strips on roasting rack in pan. □ Roast for 30 minutes. □ Turn strips over. Roast 15 minutes longer. □ Remove from oven. Brush with seasoning mixture.
- When meat is cool enough to handle, slice crosswise into ¼″ thin pieces.

- Serve warm or at room temperature with any vegetable or boiled rice. □ This roast pork also makes excellent sandwiches.

STIR-FRY PORK WITH GREEN ONIONS

A popular northern Chinese dish

Preparation time: 25 minutes   Makes 4 servings
Cooking time: 5 minutes

1½ pounds good lean pork

MARINADE:

- 1 tablespoon ketchup
- 1 tablespoon cornstarch
- 2 tablespoons soy sauce
- 1 teaspoon sugar
- 2 tablespoons cooking sherry
- 1 teaspoon salt
- ¼ teaspoon black pepper

- 1 bunch green onions (about 8)
- 4 tablespoons vegetable oil

PREPARATION:

- Cut pork into 1½″ strips along the grain and then against the grain into very thin pieces.
- Thoroughly mix pork with marinade ingredients in a large bowl and set aside for at least 15 minutes.
- Cut onion into 1″ pieces.

TO COOK:

- Heat vegetable oil in wok or large fry pan over high heat. □ Brown onions for a few seconds. □ Add marinated pork. Stir and cook for about 4 minutes. (Pork should be juicy and cooked through.) □ Remove from heat.
- Serve hot.

BARBEQUED PORK RIBS

It's better to bake individual ribs than it is to bake whole long strips of ribs because more fat is rendered.

Preparation time: 20 minutes   Makes 4 servings
Marinating time: 30 minutes
Cooking time: 1 hour 45 minutes

3 pounds pork ribs

SAUCE:

3 tablespoons ketchup
2 tablespoons cooking
   sherry
3 tablespoons soy sauce
1 tablespoon sugar
1 teaspoon sesame oil
¼ teaspoon ginger powder
¼ teaspoon black pepper
¼ teaspoon garlic powder
½ teaspoon salt

PREPARATION:

- Cut strips of ribs into individual ribs.
- Mix sauce ingredients well in a small bowl. □ Put ribs in a large bowl and pour sauce over them. Rub the sauce over the ribs. □ Marinate at least 30 minutes.

TO COOK:

- Preheat oven to 325°F. □ Put the ribs on a cookie sheet. Bake 45 minutes. □ Turn ribs over. Continue baking 45 minutes longer. □ Turn ribs over again. Increase oven temperature to 350°. Bake 15 minutes longer. □ Transfer to serving plate rib by rib so that the grease will remain in the pan.

- Serve hot or warm.

STIR-FRY SPARERIBS

Onion, soy sauce, and sherry flavor this dish.

Preparation time: 20 minutes

Cooking time: 40 minutes

Makes 4 servings

---

3 pounds lean and meaty
   spareribs
1 medium onion
2 tablespoons vegetable oil
½ cup water
4 tablespoons soy sauce
2 teaspoons sugar
1 teaspoon salt
¼ teaspoon black pepper
2 tablespoons cooking
   sherry
1 tablespoon cornstarch
   dissolved in 2 tablespoons
   water

PREPARATION:

■ Have the butcher cut ribs crosswise into three strips. At home, cut ribs into 2 ″ chunks. Rinse ribs. Dry with paper towels. □ Chop onion.

TO COOK:

■ Heat vegetable oil in wok or large fry pan over high heat. □ Brown onion for a few seconds. □ Add ribs. Cook and stir over high heat, browning ribs for 3 to 4 minutes. □ Add water, soy sauce, sugar, salt, black pepper, and cooking sherry. Bring to a boil. □ Cover and cook over medium-low heat until the ribs are tender, about 30 minutes. Stir occasionally. □ Push ribs to sides of pan. Add dissolved cornstarch to liquid in center. Stir and cook a few seconds until sauce is slightly thickened. □ Mix well with ribs, skim off any excess fat.

■ Serve over boiled or steamed rice with Quick-Cooked Mixed Vegetables (page 97).

SPICY TWICE-COOKED PORK

A very popular family-style Szechuan dish

Preparation time: 40 minutes   Makes 4 servings
Cooking time: 5 minutes

SAUCE:
   2 teaspoons ketchup
   2½ tablespoons soy sauce
   1 tablespoon cooking sherry
   1 teaspoon sesame oil
   1½ teaspoons sugar
   ¼ teaspoon salt

   3 cloves garlic
   2 small (or 1 large) green
      pepper
   ½ cup onion, cut in 1″ square
      pieces
   1 pound lean pork in two
      pieces
   3 tablespoons vegetable oil
      dried red chili peppers (2
      or 3)
   ½ cup canned sliced bamboo
      shoots

PREPARATION:
- Mix sauce ingredients in a small bowl and set aside.
- Peel and lightly crush garlic. □ Remove seeds and stem from green pepper and discard. □ Cut pepper and onion into 1″ square pieces.

TO COOK:
- Put pork and enough water to cover in a small, deep saucepan. Bring to a boil over high heat. □ Lower heat to medium. Cook 8 to 10 minutes. Remove pork from pan and let cool. □ Slice cooled pork against the grain into very thin 1½″ pieces.
- Heat vegetable oil in wok or large fry pan over high heat. □ Add garlic and red peppers and brown until they turn dark. (You may discard the garlic and red peppers, if you wish.) □ Add onions, green peppers, and bamboo shoots. Stir and cook about 30 seconds. □ Add boiled sliced pork. Cook and stir about 30 seconds. □ Add sauce. Cook and stir for about 45 seconds to 1 minute longer.
- Serve hot.

CHINESE-STYLE PORK CHOPS

In Shanghai, a bowl of noodle soup is served topped with this tender and tasty pork chop.

Preparation time: 25 minutes   Makes 4 servings
Marinating time: 1 hour
Cooking time: 25 minutes

**8 center-cut pork loin chops,
¼″ to ½″ thick**

MARINADE:

**2 tablespoons soy sauce
2 tablespoons cooking
   sherry
1 teaspoon salt
1 teaspoon sugar
¼ teaspoon black pepper**

**1 tablespoon cornstarch
1 cup vegetable oil**

PREPARATION:

- Using the back of a cleaver or heavy knife, pound the pork chops lengthwise from one end to the other and then crosswise from one end to the other. Turn chops over and repeat. (This makes them thinner and more tender.)
- Mix marinade ingredients in a large bowl. □ Add pork chops, rubbing sauce onto chops. Marinate at room temperature at least 1 hour. □ Drain liquid from chops and dry with paper towels. □ Sprinkle a little cornstarch on both sides of each chop. Using index finger, lightly rub cornstarch over the chops. (The cornstarch seals in the juices, preventing the meat from becoming dry and tough.) Set aside.

TO COOK:

- Preheat oven to low. □ Heat vegetable oil in wok or large fry pan over high heat. □ When the oil is very hot, drop two chops into the pan. (Using 1 cup of oil and frying only two chops at a time provides better browning than using a lot of oil and frying all chops at once.) Fry until both sides are brown, about 5 minutes. □ Remove from pan and keep warm on a cookie sheet in oven. □ Repeat frying, two chops at a time. (Total frying time — 20 minutes)
- Serve hot or warm with vegetables and rice.

"LION'S HEAD" MEATBALLS AND CABBAGE

A popular Chinese casserole dish in which the meatballs are big and rough and resemble a lion's head

Preparation time: 25 minutes   Makes 4 servings
Cooking time: 45 minutes

1 small head cabbage (about 1 pound)

1½ pounds lean ground pork

MARINADE:

2 eggs
2 tablespoons finely chopped green onion
2 tablespoons cooking sherry
2 tablespoons cornstarch

2 tablespoons soy sauce
½ teaspoon salt
½ teaspoon sugar
¼ teaspoon ginger powder
¼ teaspoon white or black pepper

4 tablespoons vegetable oil
2 tablespoons soy sauce
1 teaspoon sugar
½ teaspoon salt

1 cup water
1 tablespoon cornstarch dissolved in 3 tablespoons water

PREPARATION:

- Core cabbage and cut into 2″ pieces. Set aside.
- Thoroughly mix marinade ingredients with pork in a large bowl. Mix with a fork for at least 2 minutes. □ Divide into four balls. Using hands, pack each ball tightly. The best way to do this is to toss meatball lightly from hand to hand until it is well formed.

TO COOK:

- Heat vegetable oil in a large (10″) pot over medium-high heat. □ Brown the four meatballs on all sides for about 5 minutes. (Insides will still be raw.) □ Transfer to a plate and set aside. □ Drain most of the fat, leaving 2 tablespoons in the pot. □ Add cabbage. Cook and stir 1 to 2 minutes. □ Add soy sauce, sugar, and salt. Cook and stir 1 to 2 minutes more. □ Add the water. Stir well. □ Put the meatballs on top of cabbage. Lower heat to medium-low. Cover and cook about 20 minutes. □ Turn meatballs over. Cook another 10 minutes, covered. □ Push meatballs and cabbage to sides of pot. □ Add dissolved cornstarch to liquid in center. Stir until sauce has thickened slightly. Mix well with cabbage and meatballs. Remove from heat.

- To serve, put cabbage on a large plate with meatballs on top. □ Hot boiled rice is good with this dish.

POULTRY

鶏或鴨

To catch a chicken you must have two grains of rice.

CHINESE PROVERB

NOTES

STIR-FRY CHICKEN

This is the traditional and most popular way of cooking chicken Chinese-style. The chicken is cut into chunks before cooking to get more flavor from the meat and to make it easy to eat with chopsticks.

Preparation time: 20 minutes   Makes 4 servings
Cooking time: 25 minutes

SAUCE:

>   3 tablespoons soy sauce
>   1 tablespoon cooking sherry
>   1 teaspoon sugar
>   ½ teaspoon salt
>   ½ teaspoon ginger powder
>   (or 1 teaspoon finely
>   chopped gingerroot)

>   chicken parts
>   (2½-3 pounds)
>   2 tablespoons chopped
>   onion
>   2 tablespoons vegetable oil
>   cornstarch (for sauce, if
>   needed)

PREPARATION:

■ Combine sauce ingredients in a small bowl and set aside.

■ Cut chicken into small serving pieces (cut legs in half, breasts in thirds, etc.).

■ Chop onion.

TO COOK:

■ Heat vegetable oil in wok or large fry pan over high heat. □ Brown onion for a few seconds. □ Add chicken pieces and cook and stir for about 2 minutes. □ Lower heat and add sauce. Cook and stir about 1 minute over low heat. □ Cover pan and cook about 10 minutes. □ Remove cover and cook 5 minutes longer. (The chicken should be tender but not falling apart.) □ If there is more than ½ cup of liquid in the pan, push chicken to the sides and add 2 tablespoons cornstarch dissolved in 2 tablespoons water to the liquid in the center of pan. Stir sauce until slightly thickened and mix well with chicken.

■ Serve with hot, boiled rice.

CORNISH HENS WITH SAVORY RICE STUFFING

Very nice for a dinner party, this tasty and filling dish needs only a salad to go with it. The sauce may seem too salty, but it's really not when it's combined with the hens.

Preparation time: 40 minutes   Makes 4 servings
Cooking time: 1 hour 25 minutes

STUFFING:

1 cup round-grain rice
1 cup water
4 strips bacon
3 tablespoons chopped onion
2 cups sliced fresh mushrooms
½ cup frozen peas, thawed
2 tablespoons soy sauce
1 teaspoon sugar
1 teaspoon sesame oil
½ teaspoon salt

4 Cornish hens (about 1 pound 4 ounces each)
2 tablespoons cooking sherry mixed with 1 tablespoon salt

SAUCE:

1 teaspoon sugar
2 teaspoons cornstarch dissolved in 2 tablespoons water
1 cup liquid from roasting pan

■ Put rice in a small, deep saucepan. Cover with tap water. Stir several times with spoon or with your hand. Drain and repeat washing process at least twice. Drain well. □ Bring drained rice and the cup of water to boil in saucepan. Boil 2 minutes with cover slightly ajar. □ Remove from heat, cover and let stand at least 10 minutes. (Rice will be half-cooked, and the liquid should be almost absorbed.)

■ Chop bacon and onion. □ Slice mushrooms.

■ Cook and stir chopped bacon in wok or large fry pan over medium-high heat for about 1½ minutes or just until the bacon begins to crisp. □ Add onions and mushrooms and cook and stir about 30 seconds. □ Add peas. Cook and stir a few seconds more. □ Add half-cooked rice. Stir. □ Add soy sauce, sugar, sesame oil, and salt. Stir well and cook about 1 minute. Remove from heat and set aside.

■ Preheat oven to 450°F. □ Remove giblets from hens. Rinse and remove fat from backs of hens. Chop off small ends of wings and discard. Dry hens well with paper towels. □ Pack the cavity of each hen tightly with stuffing. □ Rub the outsides of the hens with the sherry and salt mixture. (Use all the mixture for the four hens.)

- Put hens in a roasting pan with a piece of tin foil on the bottom to prevent sticking. Roast uncovered for 20 minutes. □ Lower oven temperature to 325° F., cover tightly with foil and continue cooking for 1 hour.
- Transfer hens to a serving platter. □ Pour liquid (about 1 cup) from roasting pan into a small saucepan. □ Add remaining sugar. Bring to a quick boil. □ Add dissolved cornstarch and cook and stir until slightly thickened. Pour sauce over hens.
- Spoon some sauce over each individual hen and serve.

MARINATED BAKED CHICKEN

This easy dish is attractive served on a bed of a few lettuce leaves garnished with fresh parsley.

Preparation time: 10 minutes

Makes 4 servings

Marinating time: 4 hours or overnight

Cooking time: 1 hour

frying chicken parts (2½–3 pounds)
cloves garlic (2 or 3)
¼ teaspoon ginger powder (or ½ teaspoon finely chopped gingerroot)
2½ tablespoons soy sauce
1 teaspoon sugar
1 tablespoon cooking sherry
½ teaspoon salt

PREPARATION:
- Arrange chicken pieces in a large bowl.
- Peel and crush garlic. □ Mix with remaining ingredients in a small bowl and pour over chicken. Turn each piece to coat well with sauce.
- Cover and refrigerate at least 4 hours or overnight. □ Turn pieces at least once.

TO COOK:
- Preheat oven to 400° F. □ Line a large pan with tinfoil (for easy cleanup). Arrange chicken pieces in pan. □ Bake 30 minutes. □ Turn chicken pieces over and continue to bake 30 minutes longer.
- Serve hot.

CHICKEN BREASTS WITH MUSHROOMS AND ZUCCHINI

A light and flavorful combination

Preparation time: 30 minutes

Cooking time: 5 minutes

Makes 4 servings

2 whole chicken breasts (6-8 ounces each)

MARINADE:
1 tablespoon cooking sherry
1 tablespoon soy sauce
1 teaspoon cornstarch
½ teaspoon sugar

½ medium (or 1 small) zucchini
2 tablespoons chopped onion
1 cup sliced fresh mushrooms

4 tablespoons vegetable oil
½ teaspoon salt
1 teaspoon soy sauce
1 teaspoon sesame oil
⅛ teaspoon black pepper

PREPARATION:

■ Bone and skin chicken breasts. Cut each breast in half lengthwise. Remove gristle. Cut in half lengthwise again. Tilt your knife blade slightly away from you and slice into very thin pieces against the grain.

■ Mix chicken well with marinade ingredients and set aside.

■ Cut zucchini in half lengthwise and then slice crosswise into ¼ " slices. □ Chop onion. □ Slice mushrooms.

TO COOK:

■ Heat 3 tablespoons of the vegetable oil in wok or large fry pan over high heat. □ Brown onion for a few seconds. □ Add chicken and cook and stir until the color changes and the meat is cooked through, about 2 minutes. □ Transfer chicken to a bowl. □ Add the remaining vegetable oil to pan. □ Add the mushrooms and zucchini and cook and stir over medium-high heat for a few seconds. □ Add salt, soy sauce, sesame oil, and black pepper. Cook and stir about 30 seconds. □ Put chicken back in pan. Mix well with vegetables and cook and stir for about 30 seconds longer.

■ Serve immediately.

CHICKEN IN HOT SAUCE

Spicy hot—Szechuan-style chicken

Preparation time: 30 minutes

Cooking time: 5 minutes

Makes 4 servings

SAUCE:

- 1 tablespoon soy sauce
- 2 tablespoons water
- 1 teaspoon vinegar
- 1 teaspoon sugar
- ¼ teaspoon ginger powder (or ½ teaspoon finely chopped gingerroot)
- ¼ teaspoon garlic powder (or ½ teaspoon finely chopped fresh garlic)
- ¼ teaspoon salt
- 1 teaspoon cornstarch
- 1 teaspoon sesame oil

MARINADE:

- 2 teaspoons cornstarch
- 1 tablespoon soy sauce
- 1 tablespoon cooking sherry
- ½ teaspoon sugar

- 1 small green pepper
- 2 tablespoons chopped onion
- 4 tablespoons vegetable oil
- 3-4 dried red chili peppers
- ½ cup dry roasted peanuts

2 whole chicken breasts (6-8 ounces each)

PREPARATION:

- Mix sauce ingredients in a small bowl and set aside.
- Bone and skin chicken breasts and cut in ½" cubes.
- Mix chicken cubes well with marinade ingredients and set aside.
- Remove stem and seeds from green pepper and discard. Cut pepper in ½" pieces. □ Chop onion. Set aside.

TO COOK:

- Heat vegetable oil in wok or large fry pan over high heat. □ Add dried red peppers and brown for a few seconds. When the peppers turn dark, discard. □ Add onion and brown for a few seconds. □ Add marinated chicken. Cook and stir about 2 minutes. □ Add green pepper. Cook and stir about 1 more minute. □ Add peanuts, stir, and add sauce. Cook about 45 seconds longer.

- Serve piping hot.

PUNGENT GREEN ONION CHICKEN

When this dish is served in China, the chicken pieces, including the feet and head, are arranged on the platter to resemble a live chicken!

Preparation time: 30 minutes
Cooking time: 35 minutes

Makes 4 servings

> whole frying chicken (2½–3 pounds)
> 1 tablespoon cooking sherry
> 1 tablespoon salt
> ½ cup sliced green onion
> 1 cup water
> 1 tablespoon sesame oil
> 1 tablespoon vegetable oil

PREPARATION:

- Trim any excess fat from chicken. Wash and dry with paper towels. □ Rub with sherry and then with salt inside and out.
- Cut onion in 2″ pieces and then in slivers lengthwise.

TO COOK:

- Bring water to boil in large pot. □ Put in chicken, breast side up. Cover and cook over medium heat 20 minutes. (Chicken should be tender but not falling apart.) □ Remove from pot to cool. *Reserve liquid* (about ½ cup).
- When the chicken is cool enough to handle, cut into 2″ serving pieces with cleaver or large butcher knife. (First remove legs. Cut each in half. Remove wings. Remove thighs and cut each in half. Cut off back. Cut into pieces. Cut breasts in half and then each half in thirds.)
- Arrange attractively (back parts under breasts) on serving platter. □ Put onions in a pile on top of chicken in the center of the platter.
- Heat vegetable and sesame oils together in a small pot over high heat. □ When the oils are very hot and begin to smoke, slowly and evenly pour over pile of green onions. Carefully drain as much oil as possible from the platter back into the pot. □ Add reserved liquid to pot. Bring to boil. Boil about 10 seconds. □ Pour over onions and chicken pieces. Spread the onions around the chicken.

- Serve warm. (Can be reheated in oven.)

ALMOND CHICKEN

A popular dish invented by Chinese in America

Preparation time: 25 minutes   Makes 4 servings
Cooking time: 5 minutes

2 whole chicken breasts (6-8 ounces each)

MARINADE:
1 tablespoon soy sauce
2 teaspoons cornstarch
1 teaspoon sugar

SAUCE:
2 tablespoons soy sauce
1 tablespoon cooking sherry
1 teaspoon cornstarch
1 teaspoon sesame oil
1 teaspoon vinegar
1 teaspoon sugar
¼ teaspoon ginger powder
¼ teaspoon garlic powder
dash Tabasco pepper sauce

2 green onions
3 tablespoons vegetable oil
1 package (3⅛ ounces) whole blanched almonds

PREPARATION:
- Bone and skin chicken breasts. Cut into ½" cubes.
- Mix marinade ingredients with chicken and set aside. □ Mix sauce ingredients in a small bowl and set aside.
- Cut green onions in 1" pieces.

TO COOK:
- Heat vegetable oil in wok or large fry pan over high heat. □ Add almonds. Stir and brown for about 1 minute. *Do not burn.* Remove almonds from pan and set aside. (Reserve oil in pan.) □ Add onion and brown for a few seconds. □ Add marinated chicken. Cook and stir about 2 minutes. □ Add almonds. Add sauce. Cook and stir 30 seconds longer.
- Serve immediately.

LEMON CHICKEN

With its fresh, sweet-sour taste, this dish is more an American favorite than a traditional Chinese dish.

Preparation time: 30 minutes   Makes 4 servings
Cooking time: 4 minutes

**2 whole chicken breasts
(about 12 ounces meat)**

MARINADE:
1 egg
1 tablespoon soy sauce
1 teaspoon cornstarch
1 teaspoon flour
½ teaspoon sugar
¼ teaspoon salt

SAUCE:
**3½ tablespoons fresh lemon
juice**
3 tablespoons sugar
½ teaspoon salt
3 tablespoons water
2 teaspoons cornstarch

1 medium carrot
3 tablespoons vegetable oil

PREPARATION:
■ Bone and skin chicken breasts. Cut each breast lengthwise into four strips. Tilt knife away from you and slice each strip crosswise into very thin 1½″ pieces.

■ Mix chicken with marinade ingredients in a bowl and set aside.

■ Mix sauce ingredients in a small bowl and set aside.

■ Peel carrot and cut lengthwise in half. Cut each half crosswise into thin slices.

TO COOK:
■ Heat vegetable oil in wok or large fry pan over high heat. □ Add chicken. Cook and stir for about 1 minute. □ Add carrot slices. Cook and stir about 1 minute more. □ Add sauce. Mix well and cook and stir for 30 to 45 seconds longer. When the chicken and carrots are well coated with sauce, remove from heat.

■ Serve hot.

GARLIC CHICKEN WITH VEGETABLES

This dish is often served in Hunan-style restaurants.

Preparation time: 30 minutes
Cooking time: 5 minutes

Makes 4 servings

2 whole chicken breasts (6-8 ounces each)

MARINADE:
1 tablespoon soy sauce
1 teaspoon sugar
1 tablespoon cooking sherry
2 teaspoons cornstarch

SAUCE:
1½ tablespoons soy sauce
1 tablespoon water
½ teaspoon salt
1 tablespoon ketchup
⅛ teaspoon black pepper

cloves garlic (3 or 4)
1 medium green pepper
1 can (8½ ounces) water chestnuts, drained
2 tablespoons chopped onion
3 tablespoons vegetable oil
1 can (8½ ounces) sliced bamboo shoots, drained

PREPARATION:

- Bone and skin chicken breasts. Cut in half lengthwise. Remove gristle. Cut in half lengthwise again. Tilt knife away from you and slice against the grain into thin 1″ pieces.
- Mix sliced chicken with marinade ingredients in a bowl and set aside. □ Mix sauce ingredients well in a small bowl and set aside.
- Peel garlic and chop fine. □ Remove stem and seeds from green pepper and discard. Cut pepper into 1″ pieces. □ Cut water chestnuts horizontally into ¼″ slices. □ Chop onion.

TO COOK:

- Heat vegetable oil in wok or large fry pan over high heat. □ Brown onion and garlic for a few seconds. □ Add chicken. Stir and cook about 1½ minutes. □ Add green pepper, bamboo shoots, and water chestnuts. Stir and cook 30 seconds. □ Add sauce. Stir and cook 2 minutes longer. Remove from heat.

- Serve hot.

DEEP-FRIED CHICKEN— CHINESE-STYLE

Marinating the chicken first adds flavor to this easy dish.

Preparation time: 15 minutes

Marinating time: 4 hours

Cooking time: 30 minutes

Makes 2 to 4 servings

2½-3 pounds chicken parts

MARINADE:
2 tablespoons soy sauce
1 tablespoon cooking sherry
1 teaspoon sugar
1 teaspoon sesame oil
1 teaspoon salt
¼ teaspoon ginger powder
¼ teaspoon black pepper

3 cups vegetable oil
½ cup flour

PREPARATION:

■ Rinse chicken and dry with paper towels.

■ Mix chicken parts with marinade ingredients in a large bowl. □ Cover and marinate in refrigerator for at least 4 hours, turning pieces occasionally.

TO COOK:

■ Preheat oven to low. □ Heat vegetable oil in wok or large fry pan over high heat.

■ Lightly coat marinated chicken pieces with flour. □ When the oil is hot, deep-fry chicken, a few pieces at a time, until golden brown and crisp (about 15 minutes). □ Keep fried pieces in warm oven until ready to serve.

■ Serve hot.

COLD GARLIC-FLAVORED CHICKEN

In Chinese restaurants, thinly sliced chicken breasts seasoned with sesame sauce and bean sprouts are served cold. Easier to prepare and very tasty, the version presented here can be prepared several hours before serving and keeps well in the refrigerator.

Preparation time: 25 minutes   Makes 4 servings
Cooking time: 25 minutes

2½-3 pounds chicken parts
   2 tablespoons cooking
     sherry
1½ teaspoons salt
    cloves garlic (3 or 4)
   1 cup water

SAUCE:
  ½ cup chicken stock (re-
    served from boiled
    chicken)
  1 tablespoon vinegar
  ½ teaspoon salt
  ¼ teaspoon black pepper
  2 teaspoons soy sauce

   1 tablespoon sesame oil

■ Wash chicken parts and dry with paper towels. □ Mix sherry and salt and rub over chicken. Set aside.
■ Peel and crush garlic and set aside.
■ Bring water to boil over high heat in a large pot with a cover. □ Add chicken parts. Lower heat to medium. Cover and cook 15 minutes. □ Remove chicken to a plate and let cool. □ Skim as much fat as possible from stock and reserve ½ cup stock.
■ Mix the reserved stock with sauce ingredients in a small bowl and set aside.
■ Using a heavy knife, cut chicken into 2″ serving pieces. Put in a large bowl.
■ Heat sesame oil in a small saucepan over high heat. □ Add crushed garlic. Stir and brown for a few seconds. □ Add the sauce mixture and boil for about 30 seconds. Remove from heat immediately. Discard garlic. □ Pour hot sauce over cut-up chicken. Stir gently, coating pieces well.
■ Arrange chicken on a serving plate. □ Pour any sauce left in bowl over chicken pieces. □ Cover with tinfoil. □ Refrigerate at least 30 minutes.

■ Serve cold.

CRISPY DUCK WITH ORANGE SAUCE

As a change from the French cognac and butter sauce, try this light and fresh Chinese way to prepare duck.

Preparation time: 30 minutes
Cooking time: 2½ hours

Makes 4 servings

SAUCE:
    1 tablespoon soy sauce
    1 tablespoon ketchup
    2 tablespoons sugar
    2 teaspoons vinegar
    1 cup orange juice

SEASONING MIXTURE:
    2 tablespoons cooking
      sherry
    1 tablespoon brown sugar
    1 teaspoon salt

---

    1 frozen duckling (4-4½
      pounds), thawed
    1 tablespoon sesame oil
    1½ tablespoons cornstarch
      dissolved in 3 tablespoons
      water
      orange slices for garnish

PREPARATION:
- Preheat oven to 325° F.
- Mix sauce ingredients in a small bowl. Set aside.
- Wash duckling and dry with paper towels. Discard small tips of wings. □ Combine seasoning ingredients and rub over duck, inside and out. □ Place duck on a rack in a roasting pan, breast side up.

TO COOK:
- Bake 1 hour. □ Drain fat. Turn duck over. Bake 1 hour more. □ Remove from oven. Let stand until cool enough to handle.*

- Using a heavy knife, cut duck into 2″ serving pieces. (Remove legs. Cut each in half. Remove wings. Remove thighs and cut in half. Cut off back. Cut into pieces. Cut breasts in half and then each half in thirds.)
- Increase oven heat to 450°. Put duck pieces on a cookie sheet, skin side up. Brown in oven for about 20 minutes. □ Meanwhile, heat sesame oil in a small saucepan over high heat. □ When the oil is hot, add sauce mixture. Bring to a boil. Boil for a few seconds. □ Add dissolved cornstarch. Cook and stir until the sauce is slightly thickened. Remove from heat.
- Arrange browned duck pieces attractively on a serving plate. □ Pour the hot sauce over the duck. □ Garnish with orange slices.
- Serve immediately, spooning some sauce over individual servings.

*Note: The duck can be cooked this far in advance. Just before serving cut into pieces as directed and brown in 450° oven for 20 minutes. Prepare sauce, arrange pieces on platter and pour sauce over duck.

CURRIED CHICKEN

A curry recipe is not usually found in a Chinese cookbook, but I found that when cooking Chinese pan-fried chicken, the addition of curry powder gives it an excellent flavor.

Preparation time: 25 minutes

Cooking time: 25 minutes

Makes 4 servings

> frying chicken parts (2½-3 pounds)
> 2 large potatoes
> 3 tablespoons chopped onion
> 2 tablespoons vegetable oil
> 2 tablespoons soy sauce
> 1 teaspoon sugar
> ½ teaspoon ginger powder
> ½ teaspoon salt
> 1 tablespoon curry powder
> ½ cup water

PREPARATION:

■ Cut chicken parts into small serving pieces. (Cut legs in half, breasts in thirds, etc.) □ Peel potato and cut in chunks. □ Chop onion.

TO COOK:

■ Heat vegetable oil in a large, deep skillet over high heat. □ Brown onion for a few seconds. □ Add chicken pieces and cook and stir for about 2 minutes. □ When slightly brown, lower heat to medium and add soy sauce, sugar, and ginger powder. Cover and cook about 5 minutes. □ Add potatoes, salt, curry powder, and water. Stir well. Lower heat, cover and simmer 12 to 15 minutes. Stir occasionally to prevent potatoes from sticking to the bottom of the pan.

■ Serve over hot rice.

ROAST DUCK WITH SPICY SAUCE

Ducks are very fatty. In this recipe, the duck is cooked on a rack in a broiler pan. So much oil will drain from the duck as it cooks that it will be necessary to empty the pan while the duck is roasting.

Preparation time: 30 minutes
Cooking time: 2½ hours

Makes 4 servings

frozen duckling (4-4½ pounds) thawed

SEASONING MIXTURE:
1 tablespoon cooking sherry
1 teaspoon vinegar
1 teaspoon sesame oil
1 tablespoon brown sugar
1 teaspoon salt

SAUCE:
½ cup water
1 tablespoon cooking sherry
3 tablespoons soy sauce
1 teaspoon sesame oil
½ teaspoon salt
2 teaspoons sugar
chopped green onion (2 or 3 tablespoons)
1 dried red chili pepper, crushed (about 1 teaspoon)

PREPARATION:
- Preheat oven to 300° F. Rinse duck well. Dry with paper towels. Remove as much excess fat as possible. □ Mix seasoning ingredients well and rub on duck, inside and out. □ Mix sauce ingredients in a small saucepan. Set aside.

TO COOK:
- Put duck on a rack in a broiler pan and bake 1 hour. □ Drain fat from pan. Turn duck over. Bake 1 hour more. □ Turn oven temperature to 375°. Brown duck for 10 minutes. □ Remove from oven and let cool.
- When duck is cool enough to handle, cut into 2″ serving pieces with a large, heavy knife. (First remove legs. Cut each in half. Remove wings. Remove thighs and cut in half. Cut off back. Cut into pieces. Cut breasts in half and then each half in thirds.)
- Arrange duck attractively (back parts under breast pieces) on a serving platter.
- Heat sauce and bring to a full boil. □ Remove from heat. Pour evenly over duck. □ Carefully drain sauce from platter back into pan. Bring to a second boil. □ Pour sauce evenly over duck.
- Serve warm.

SEAFOOD

海鮮

If you cannot catch fish, catch shrimps.

CHINESE PROVERB

NOTES

SZECHUAN-STYLE RED SNAPPER

The Chinese province of Szechuan is known for its spicy food, especially seafood. Spices such as ginger, garlic and dried red chili peppers are used to disguise the strong fish odors.

Preparation time: 20 minutes   Makes 3 to 4 servings
Cooking time: 12 minutes

SAUCE:

2 tablespoons soy sauce
1 teaspoon sugar
½ teaspoon ginger powder
½ teaspoon garlic powder
½ teaspoon salt
¼ teaspoon crushed dried red chili pepper
1 tablespoon chopped onion
1 tablespoon cooking sherry
1 teaspoon vinegar
1 teaspoon sesame oil
3 tablespoons water

1 pound red snapper fillets
flour
2 tablespoons vegetable oil
2 teaspoons cornstarch dissolved in 2 tablespoons water
fresh parsley for garnish (if desired)

PREPARATION:

- Mix sauce ingredients in a small bowl and set aside.
- Cut fish fillets into 2″ pieces. □ Coat each piece of fish with flour.

TO COOK:

- Heat vegetable oil in a large fry pan over medium-high heat. Brown both sides of fish pieces lightly. □ Pour sauce over fish. Bring to a boil. □ Cook and stir gently over high heat about 1½ minutes. □ Push fish to sides of pan. □ Add dissolved cornstarch to liquid in center. Stir liquid and cook a few seconds until slightly thickened. □ Mix well with fish. Garnish with chopped fresh parsley, if desired.

- Serve immediately.

FISH WITH GREEN PEPPERS

This dish is served often as part of a Cantonese brunch.

Preparation time: 35 minutes
Cooking time: 8 minutes

Makes 4 servings

FISH PASTE:

10 ounces fillet of sole (or
    any other firm-fleshed fish)
4 ounces ground pork
1 egg
2 tablespoons cooking
    sherry

1 teaspoon salt
1 teaspoon sugar
1 teaspoon sesame oil
1 tablespoon cornstarch

3 large green peppers
3 tablespoons vegetable oil
1 cup water
2 tablespoons soy sauce
2 teaspoons sugar

⅛ teaspoon black pepper
1½ tablespoons cornstarch
    dissolved in 4 tablespoons
    water

PREPARATION:

- Cut fish into small chunks.
- Mix fish paste ingredients well and grind in a blender or blend in a food processor until the mixture becomes a thick paste.
- Cut peppers lengthwise into quarters. Remove stems and seeds. Cut each quarter in half, making twenty-four pieces.
- Put 1 tablespoon of the fish paste on each green pepper square. Pack tightly. Repeat, using all paste.

TO COOK:

- Heat 2 tablespoons vegetable oil in wok or large fry pan over medium-high heat. Tilt pan and coat well with the oil. □ Drop in about half of the fish-paste pepper squares, paste side down. Brown about 1 minute. □ Remove carefully from the pan and put on a plate, paste side up. □ Add the remaining vegetable oil to pan. Drop in remaining squares, paste side down. Brown 1 minute. □ Turn squares over. □ Add browned squares from plate, paste side up. □ Add ½ cup water. Cover and bring to boil. Boil 2 minutes. □ Remove from heat. Carefully transfer all squares to a plate, paste side up. □ Add the remaining water to pan. Add soy sauce, sugar, and black pepper and bring to boil. □ Add dissolved cornstarch. Stir for a few seconds until sauce is clear and thickened. Pour evenly over fish squares.
- Serve immediately.

SWEET AND SOUR FISH

In a Mandarin-style restaurant, the whole fish is deep-fried and served with a sweet-sour sauce.

Preparation time: 25 minutes   Makes 4 servings
Cooking time: 20 minutes

BATTER:
  2 eggs
  ½ cup cornstarch
  1 teaspoon salt
  2 tablespoons water

SAUCE:
  1 cup water
  3 tablespoons sugar
  2 tablespoons vinegar
  3 tablespoons ketchup
  1 teaspoon soy sauce

  1 pound fillet of sole (or any
    other firm white fish)
    vegetable oil (2 or 3 cups)
  2 cloves garlic
  1 tablespoon cornstarch
    dissolved in 2 tablespoons
    water

PREPARATION:

■ Beat eggs and mix thoroughly with other batter ingredients in a bowl and set aside. □ Mix sauce ingredients in a bowl and set aside.
■ Rinse fish and dry with paper towels. □ Cut in 2″ pieces. □ Peel and crush garlic. Set aside.

TO COOK:

■ Preheat oven to 300°F.
■ Heat vegetable oil in wok or large fry pan over high heat. □ Coat fish pieces with batter. □ Drop one piece at a time into the hot oil. Fry a few pieces at a time until lightly browned. □ Transfer to a cookie sheet and keep hot in oven. Repeat until all fish pieces are fried. □ Remove oil from pan, leaving 1 tablespoon. Heat the remaining oil and brown the crushed garlic for a few seconds over high heat. □ When the garlic turns dark, add sauce and bring to a boil. □ Discard garlic. Add dissolved cornstarch. Stir well until the sauce is clear and thickened. □ Immediately add fried fish and mix well. □ Remove from heat. The fish may not be crisp but will be very tasty.

■ Serve immediately.

BATTER-FRIED FISH FILLETS

Baking soda makes a tender and light batter. Fried fish should be eaten sprinkled with black pepper and dipped in vinegar.

Preparation time: 15 minutes

Cooking time: 10 minutes

Makes 4 servings

BATTER:
- **1 cup all-purpose flour**
- **½ teaspoon baking soda**
- **1½ teaspoons salt**
- **1 egg**
- **½ cup plus 2 tablespoons water**
- **1 tablespoon vegetable oil**

- **1 pound fillet of sole**
- **½ cup vegetable oil for frying**
- **vinegar**
- **black pepper**

PREPARATION:

- Cut fish into 2″ pieces.
- Combine flour, baking soda, and salt in a bowl. □ Beat egg with water and vegetable oil. □ Add to dry ingredients and stir well.

TO COOK:

- Heat vegetable oil in wok or fry pan over high heat. □ Dip fish fillets in batter and fry on both sides until golden brown. □ Drain on paper towels.

- Serve hot with vinegar and black pepper for dipping.

STIR-FRY FISH WITH VEGETABLES

A very light and nutritious entrée

Preparation time: 25 minutes

Cooking time: 15 minutes

Makes 4 servings

---

1 pound red snapper fillets (or any other firm white fish)

MARINADE:
1 egg white
2 tablespoons cooking sherry
1 teaspoon salt

---

4 green onions
1 can (8½ ounces) water chestnuts, drained
½ cup flour
½ cup plus 2 tablespoons vegetable oil

1 can (8½ ounces) sliced bamboo shoots, drained
1 tablespoon soy sauce
1 teaspoon sugar

PREPARATION:

■ Cut fish into 2″ pieces. □ Mix marinade ingredients with fish pieces. Set aside for a few minutes.

■ Cut onions into 1″ pieces. □ Slice water chestnuts horizontally into ¼″ pieces.

■ Coat each piece of fish lightly with flour and set aside.

TO COOK:

■ Heat ½ cup of vegetable oil in wok or large fry pan over high heat. □ Add half of the fish pieces and brown on both sides, about 4 to 5 minutes. □ Remove fish from pan and set aside on a plate. Fry remaining fish pieces. □ Drain oil and wipe pan with a paper towel.

■ Add remaining vegetable oil to pan over high heat. □ Brown onion for a few seconds. □ Add water chestnuts and bamboo shoots. Cook and stir about 45 seconds. □ Add soy sauce and sugar. Stir well. □ Add cooked fish. Cook and stir all ingredients gently together for about 30 seconds longer.

■ Serve immediately.

SAUTÉED SPICY SHRIMP

Serve the shrimp in their shells, coated with spicy sauce. To get the full flavor, suck the sauce off the shrimp as you remove the shell with your teeth—using your fingers is definitely permitted.

Preparation time: 25 minutes   Makes 4 servings
Cooking time: 6 minutes

1 pound large shrimp
(about 12)

SAUCE:
½ cup water
1 tablespoon soy sauce
3 tablespoons ketchup
2 teaspoons sugar
1 teaspoon sesame oil
½ teaspoon salt
¼ teaspoon black pepper
½ teaspoon crushed dried
red chili peppers

1 medium onion
4 tablespoons vegetable oil
1 tablespoon cooking sherry

2 teaspoons cornstarch
dissolved in 3 tablespoons
cold water
chopped parsley for
garnish (if desired)

PREPARATION:

- Using small scissors, trim tails and legs of shrimp. Slit shell along top and remove black vein. Do not remove shell. □ Rinse well and pat dry with paper towels.
- Mix sauce ingredients in a small bowl and set aside.
- Cut onion in half along the grain and then slice thinly against the grain.

TO COOK:

- Heat vegetable oil in wok or large fry pan over high heat. □ Brown onion for a few seconds. □ Push onions to sides of pan and add shrimp. Add cooking sherry to shrimp. Brown both sides of shrimp for about 2 minutes. □ Pour sauce over shrimp, bring to a boil, and cook about 1 minute. □ Push shrimp to side of pan. □ Add dissolved cornstarch to liquid in center. Stir until slightly thickened and mix with shrimp and onions. □ Remove from heat.

- Serve garnished with a little chopped parsley, if desired.

STIR-FRY SHRIMP WITH PEAS

This is a very light and popular dish. In China, the shrimp are usually marinated with the egg white only, but I've found that using the whole egg gives more flavor to the dish.

Preparation time: 15 minutes

Marinating time: 15 minutes

Cooking time: 5 minutes

Makes 2 to 4 servings

12 ounces medium-size raw shrimp

MARINADE:

1 teaspoon salt
1 tablespoon cooking sherry
1 egg

2 tablespoons chopped onion
3 tablespoons vegetable oil
1 cup frozen peas, thawed
1 teaspoon sesame oil
¼ teaspoon salt

PREPARATION:

- Peel and devein shrimp. Rinse and dry with paper towels.
- Lightly beat egg. Mix marinade ingredients with shrimp. □ Cover and refrigerate for at least 15 minutes.
- Chop onion.

TO COOK:

- Heat vegetable oil in wok or fry pan over high heat. □ Brown onion for a few seconds. □ Add shrimp and cook and stir for about 3 minutes. □ When the shrimp are pink and almost done, add peas. □ Cook about 1 minute longer. □ Add sesame oil and salt and stir for a few seconds.
- Serve immediately.

STIR-FRY SHRIMP AND CHICKEN

Traditionally, this dish is made with shrimp, chicken, and abalone. It is just as delicious without the abalone, which is very expensive and hard to find.

Preparation time: 35 minutes
Cooking time: 6 minutes

Makes 4 servings

1 pound medium-size raw shrimp

1 whole chicken breast (6-8 ounces meat)

MARINADE FOR SHRIMP:
1 egg
1 tablespoon cooking sherry
¾ teaspoon salt

MARINADE FOR CHICKEN:
2 teaspoons cornstarch
2 teaspoons soy sauce
½ teaspoon sugar

2 green onions
½ pound fresh cauliflower
4 tablespoons vegetable oil
3 tablespoons water
¼ teaspoon salt
½ teaspoon sugar

PREPARATION:

- Peel and devein shrimp; wash and dry. Cut each shrimp in half. □ Mix shrimp with marinade ingredients in a bowl and set aside.
- Bone and skin chicken breast. Slice against the grain into thin 1″ pieces. Mix chicken pieces with marinade ingredients in a bowl and set aside.
- Cut onion in 1″ pieces. □ Cut cauliflower into small florets and slice thin (about 2 cups).

TO COOK:

- Heat vegetable oil in wok or large fry pan over high heat. □ Brown onion for a few seconds. □ Add chicken. Cook and stir for 30 seconds. □ Add shrimp. Cook and stir about 2 minutes. □ Remove chicken and shrimp from pan and transfer to a bowl. □ Add water and cauliflower to pan. Add salt and sugar. Stir and cook 1½ minutes. □ When the cauliflower is tender but still crisp, put chicken and shrimp back into pan. Cook and stir 30 seconds longer.
- Serve hot.

STIR-FRY SCALLOPS

In southern China, fresh scallops are rarely used. They are usually obtained dried and then cooked in soup. In most parts of the United States, however, scallops are plentiful frozen or fresh, and this is an easy and delicious way of preparing them.

Preparation time: 25 minutes

Makes 4 servings

Cooking time: 4 minutes

SAUCE:

- 1½ tablespoons soy sauce
- 1 tablespoon cooking sherry
- 1 teaspoon sugar
- ¼ teaspoon garlic powder
- ¼ teaspoon crushed dried red chili peppers
- ½ teaspoon salt
- 2 teaspoons cornstarch
- 1 teaspoon sesame oil

- 1 pound fresh or frozen scallops
- ½ cup thinly sliced onions
- 3 tablespoons vegetable oil
- ½ cup frozen peas, thawed
- ½ cup canned sliced bamboo shoots

PREPARATION:

- Mix sauce ingredients in a small bowl and set aside.
- Rinse scallops and dry with paper towels. Slice scallops horizontally in half.
- Cut onions into thin slices.

TO COOK:

- Heat vegetable oil in wok or large fry pan over high heat. □ Add scallops. Cook and stir about 1 minute. □ Add onions, peas, and bamboo shoots. Cook and stir about 1 more minute. □ Add sauce. Cook and stir about 30 seconds longer. Do not overcook the scallops — they will become too watery.

- Serve immediately.

CRACKED CRAB WITH GINGER SAUCE

A little messy eating but very tasty—this dish is as delicious as Cantonese crab in lobster sauce but a lot easier to prepare!

Preparation time: 25 minutes
Cooking time: 6 minutes

Makes 4 servings

SAUCE:

1 tablespoon soy sauce
1 tablespoon vinegar
6 tablespoons water
2 teaspoons sugar
1 teaspoon sesame oil
½ teaspoon salt
½ teaspoon ginger powder

3 pounds steamed or boiled
   crab (in the shell), cleaned
2 tablespoons vegetable oil
1 dried red chili pepper
2 tablespoons chopped
   onion
1 tablespoon cornstarch
   dissolved in 3 tablespoons
   water

PREPARATION:

- Mix sauce ingredients in a small bowl and set aside.
- Break crab claws from body. Cut in about three pieces each. Break body in half. Cut each half in four parts. Use a large knife in a hacking motion. (We used a Dungeness crab which weighed 3 pounds, so the claws and body had to be cut into serving pieces.)

TO COOK:

- Heat vegetable oil in wok or large fry pan over high heat. □ Break pepper in half and add to oil. When the pepper turns black, discard. □ Brown onion for a few seconds. □ Add sauce and bring to a boil. □ Add crab, mix well, and cook and stir for about 1½ minutes. □ Push crab pieces to sides of pan. □ Add dissolved cornstarch to sauce in center. Stir well until the sauce turns clear and thickens slightly. Mix well with crab pieces.

- Serve immediately.

DEEP-FRIED OYSTERS

Fresh oysters in southern China are very small and are usually served with soup or pan-fried. When I discovered the larger oysters in this country, I deep-fried them and found them delicious.

Preparation time: 25 minutes
Cooking time: 10 minutes

Makes 4 servings

BATTER:
- ¾ **cup flour**
- ½ **cup cornstarch**
- 1½ **teaspoons salt**
- ½ **teaspoon baking soda**
- 2 **eggs**
- ½ **cup plus 2 tablespoons water**
- 2 **tablespoons vegetable oil**

SEASONING MIXTURE:
- 1½ **teaspoons salt**
- ½ **teaspoon black pepper**

- 24 **medium to large fresh oysters, shelled**
- 1 **quart water**
- 3 **cups vegetable oil**

- Thoroughly mix batter ingredients in a bowl and set aside.
- Combine seasoning mixture ingredients in a small pan. □ Brown for about 1 minute over medium-high heat, stirring constantly. Let cool. □ Divide into four small dishes for dipping oysters. Set aside.
- Rinse oysters. □ Bring water to boil in a medium-size saucepan over high heat. □ Drop in oysters. Stir in boiling water for just a few seconds. (This removes the fishy smell.) □ Remove from heat. Drain water. Dry oysters with paper towels and set aside.
- Preheat oven to low. □ Heat vegetable oil in wok or deep-fry pan over high heat. □ Dip oysters in batter, coating well. □ Drop one at a time into hot oil. Fry a few at a time until golden brown. □ Put on a cookie sheet and keep warm in oven. Repeat until all oysters are fried.
- Serve hot. Dip each oyster into seasoning mixture as you are eating — or use ketchup for dipping, if desired.

EASY HOMESTYLE OYSTER SAUCE

This recipe can easily be cut in half if you have no use for a full jar of sauce.

Preparation time: 10 minutes
Cooking time: 12 minutes

---

1 jar (8 fluid ounces)
   medium-size fresh oysters
¾ cup water
4 tablespoons soy sauce
2 tablespoons cornstarch
   dissolved in 4 tablespoons
   water

PREPARATION:

- Drain liquid from oysters and rinse them.

TO COOK:

- Bring oysters and water to boil in a small saucepan over high heat. □ Boil uncovered 3 to 5 minutes. □ Remove from heat.
- Pour oysters and liquid into a blender or food processor. Blend for a few seconds.
- Pour oysters back into saucepan. □ Add soy sauce. □ Bring to a boil, stirring constantly for about 30 seconds. □ Add dissolved cornstarch. Cook and stir until the sauce resembles a very soft paste. □ Remove from heat. Cool. □ Pour into a jar and refrigerate.

- The sauce keeps well in the refrigerator for about one week. *Do not freeze.*

VEGETABLES & SALADS

蔬菜

*If you are willing to eat cabbage stalks,
you can accomplish a hundred affairs.*

CHINESE PROVERB

NOTES

STEAMED STUFFED CUCUMBERS

A family-style southern Chinese dish

Preparation time: 30 minutes　　　　　　　Makes 4 servings
Cooking time: 15 minutes

½ pound lean ground pork

MARINADE:

2 green onions (about 3 tablespoons, chopped)
1 egg
1½ tablespoons soy sauce
1 tablespoon cooking sherry
1 tablespoon cornstarch
2 teaspoons sesame oil
1 teaspoon sugar
½ teaspoon salt

SAUCE:

½ cup reserved juice from steamed cucumbers
½ teaspoon sugar
½ teaspoon salt
¼ teaspoon sesame oil
2 teaspoons cornstarch dissolved in 2 tablespoons water

2 large cucumbers
1 cup water

PREPARATION:

■ Finely chop onions. □ Using a fork, mix marinade ingredients with pork in a bowl and set aside.
■ Peel cucumbers. Cut lengthwise in half. Remove seeds with a spoon. Cut each half crosswise into five 2″ chunks (twenty pieces).
■ Spoon 1 tablespoon pork mixture into each cucumber chunk. Pack tightly.

TO COOK:

■ Put the water in a large 10″ pot (with cover). Place a steaming rack flat in pan. □ Put the stuffed cucumbers on the rack, meat side up. Cover pot. Bring to a boil over high heat. □ Lower heat to medium and steam 8 to 10 minutes. □ Remove pot from heat. Carefully take out the steamed cucumbers and arrange on a large platter, meat side up.
■ Pour juice from the steaming pan into a small saucepan. Skim off fat, leaving ½ cup of juice. □ Add sugar, salt, and sesame oil. Bring to a boil. □ Add dissolved cornstarch. Cook and stir until the mixture is clear and slightly thickened. □ Pour evenly over cucumbers.
■ Serve hot.

Note: This dish can be served without the sauce for a lighter taste.

STUFFED TOMATOES WITH CHICKEN AND SHRIMP

Instead of stuffing the tomatoes with pork and steaming them in a bamboo steamer in the traditional manner, these tomatoes are filled with a seasoned combination of chicken and shrimp and then cooked on top of the stove.

Preparation time: 45 minutes   Makes 4 servings
Cooking time: 8 minutes

4 large tomatoes
6 ounces raw chicken
6 ounces raw shrimp

MARINADE:

1 egg
1 teaspoon soy sauce
2 teaspoons cooking sherry
1 teaspoon cornstarch
1 teaspoon salt
½ teaspoon sugar

2 tablespoons finely
  chopped celery
2 tablespoons vegetable oil
½ cup water
2 teaspoons soy sauce
1 teaspoon sugar
1 teaspoon cornstarch dissolved in 2 tablespoons
  water
chopped green onion and
chopped parsley
(if desired)

■ Half fill a medium-size sauce pan with water. Bring to a full boil. □ Add tomatoes. Boil for 10 seconds. □ Remove tomatoes, peel the skin and cut in half. With a small spoon, carefully scoop out seeds and pulp. Set tomato halves aside. (*Note*: If you are already hungry, sprinkle some sugar on the tomato pulp and eat it!)
■ Remove all skin from chicken. □ Peel, devein and clean shrimp. □ Chop chicken and shrimp as fine as possible. □ Put in a bowl and add marinade ingredients.

- Pour mixture into a blender or food processor container and blend so it becomes a thick paste. (If using a blender, blend only half the mixture at a time.) □ Chop celery finely and stir into the chicken and shrimp paste.
- Spoon filling into each tomato half, packing tightly. Press and smooth gently with fingertips.
- Heat vegetable oil in wok or large fry pan over medium-high heat, turning the pan to coat entire surface with oil. □ Carefully place tomatoes in pan, filling side down. Brown about 1 minute. □ Add water, soy sauce, and sugar. Bring to a boil. □ Reduce heat to low, cover, and cook about 4 minutes.
- With a wide metal spatula, carefully transfer tomatoes to a serving bowl, filling side up. About ½ cup of liquid should remain in pan. If less, add a little water. Bring to a boil. □ Add dissolved corn-starch. Stir sauce until slightly thickened and clear. □ Pour over tomatoes.

- Serve, garnished if desired, with chopped green onion or chopped parsley.

SAVORY GREEN BEANS

A popular American vegetable with a Chinese flavor

Preparation time: 10 minutes   Makes 4 servings
Cooking time: 12 minutes

1 pound fresh string beans
2 tablespoons chopped onion
2 tablespoons vegetable oil
½ cup water
2 teaspoons soy sauce
½ teaspoon sugar
¾ teaspoon salt
¼ teaspoon garlic powder

PREPARATION:

■ Wash string beans, remove ends and break beans in half. □ Chop onion.

TO COOK:

■ Heat vegetable oil in wok or deep saucepan over medium-high heat. □ Brown onion for a few seconds. □ Add string beans. Stir and cook for about 30 seconds. □ Add water, soy sauce, sugar, salt, and garlic powder. Stir well. □ Bring to a boil. Boil 1 minute. □ Lower heat to medium-low and cook until beans are tender but still crisp, 8 to 10 minutes. Stir occasionally.

■ Serve hot.

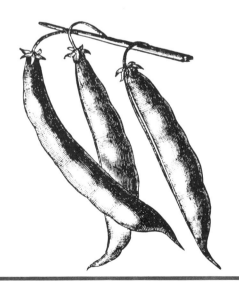

DEEP-FRIED EGGPLANT

A most delicious way of serving eggplant

Preparation time: 45 minutes Makes 4 servings
Cooking time: 20 minutes

MARINADE:

- 2 tablespoons finely chopped green onion
- 1 egg
- 2 teaspoons soy sauce
- ¾ teaspoon salt
- ½ teaspoon sugar
- 2 teaspoons sesame oil
- 2 teaspoons cornstarch

¼ pound lean ground beef

BATTER:

- ½ cup all-purpose flour
- 6 tablespoons cornstarch
- 1 egg
- 1 teaspoon salt
- ¼ teaspoon baking soda
- 1 tablespoon vegetable oil
- ½ cup plus 2 tablespoons water

1 eggplant (about 1 pound)
3 cups vegetable oil

PREPARATION:

- Chop onion. □ Thoroughly mix marinade ingredients with ground beef in a small bowl and set aside.
- Do not peel eggplant. Trim both ends and cut lengthwise into quarters. Cut each quarter crosswise into ¼" slices.
- Spoon 1 teaspoon beef mixture on a slice of eggplant. Top with another slice, aligning edges to keep triangular shape. Repeat until all the beef mixture and eggplant slices are used.

TO COOK:

- Preheat oven to low. □ Heat vegetable oil in a wok or deep-fry pan over high heat.
- Beat egg and mix with other batter ingredients. □ Dip each filled eggplant triangle into batter, coating lightly.
- Drop a few at a time into the hot oil. Fry on both sides until golden brown. □ Remove to a cookie sheet and keep warm in oven while frying remainder.
- Serve hot or warm.

EGGPLANT AND GROUND BEEF

The use of garlic and other spices in this recipe enhances the flavor of the eggplant and disguises its somewhat bitter taste.

Preparation time: 20 minutes
Cooking time: 12 minutes

Makes 4 servings

½ pound lean ground beef

MARINADE:
1 tablespoon soy sauce
½ teaspoon sugar
1 teaspoon cornstarch
½ teaspoon sesame oil

3 cloves garlic
1 eggplant (about 1 pound)
2 tablespoons vegetable oil
2 tablespoons water
1 tablespoon soy sauce
1 teaspoon sugar
½ teaspoon salt

PREPARATION:
- Mix ground beef well with marinade ingredients and set aside.
- Peel and crush garlic. □ Remove stem. Cut eggplant into bite-size chunks.

TO COOK:
- Heat vegetable oil in wok or large fry pan over high heat. □ Brown garlic for a few seconds. □ Add ground beef. Cook and stir about 1 minute. □ Add eggplant. Cook and stir for a few seconds. □ Add water and lower heat. □ Add the soy sauce, sugar, and salt. Cover and cook, stirring occasionally, until the eggplant is soft and the liquid is almost absorbed (8 to 10 minutes).
- Serve hot.

QUICK-COOKED MIXED VEGETABLES

These crunchy and delicious vegetables go well with any meat dish.

Preparation time: 30 minutes
Cooking time: 5 minutes

Makes 4 servings

SAUCE:

1 tablespoon soy sauce
1 teaspoon sugar
½ teaspoon salt
⅛ teaspoon black pepper
1 teaspoon sesame oil

water chestnuts (10 or 12, about half an 8½-ounce can)
½ pound fresh broccoli
½ medium green pepper
1 small carrot
2 large stalks celery
2 tablespoons chopped onion
3 tablespoons vegetable oil
1 tablespoon sesame seeds (if desired)

PREPARATION:

- Mix sauce ingredients in a small bowl and set aside.
- Slice water chestnuts. □ Cut broccoli into florets. □ Remove seeds and stem from green pepper and discard. Cut pepper into small strips about 1″ long and ¼″ wide. □ Peel carrot and slice thinly crosswise. □ Slice celery thinly against the grain. □ Chop onion.

TO COOK:

- Heat vegetable oil in wok or large fry pan over high heat. □ Brown onion for a few seconds. □ Add all vegetables. Lower heat slightly. Stir vegetables, coating with oil. □ Cook and stir about 1½ minutes. □ Add sauce; cook and stir until the vegetables are tender but still crisp, about 3 more minutes.
- Serve hot, sprinkled with sesame seeds, if desired.

STIR-FRY POTATOES

French fries—the Chinese way! Vinegar keeps the potatoes crisp and prevents them from becoming mushy.

Preparation time: 20 minutes   Makes 4 servings
Cooking time: 10 minutes

- 3 **large baking potatoes (about 1½ pounds)**
- 2 **green onions (about 4 tablespoons, chopped)**
- 3 **tablespoons vegetable oil**
- ½ **cup water**
- 1 **tablespoon soy sauce**
- 1 **teaspoon sugar**
- 1 **teaspoon salt**
- 2 **teaspoons vinegar**

PREPARATION:

- Peel potatoes. Slice crosswise into ¼" slices. Put three to four slices in a pile. Cut through the pile into *very thin* (¼") strips—like shoestring potatoes. (Be sure to slice the potatoes into thin strips so they will cook properly and be tasty.) ☐ Chop onions.

TO COOK:

- Heat vegetable oil in wok or large fry pan over high heat. ☐ Brown onion for a few seconds. ☐ Add potatoes. To prevent sticking, stir potatoes constantly for about 1 minute. ☐ Add water. Lower heat to medium. ☐ Add soy sauce, sugar, and salt. Cook and stir constantly for about 5 minutes. ☐ Add vinegar. Cook and stir about 2 minutes longer. The potatoes should be tender and slightly crisp.

- Serve hot.

HOT SWEET AND SOUR CABBAGE

Chili peppers and onions flavor this spicy cabbage dish.

Preparation time: 20 minutes   Makes 4 servings
Cooking time: 6 minutes

SAUCE:

- 1 tablespoon soy sauce
- 1 tablespoon vinegar
- 1 tablespoon sugar
- 1 teaspoon sesame oil
- ½ teaspoon salt

- dried red chili peppers (2 or 3)
- 2 tablespoons chopped onion
- 5 cups coarsely cut cabbage
- 3 tablespoons vegetable oil

PREPARATION:

- Mix sauce ingredients in a small bowl and set aside.
- Break chili peppers in half. □ Chop onion. □ Cut cabbage into 1½" pieces.

TO COOK:

- Heat vegetable oil in wok or large fry pan over high heat. □ Add dried red chili peppers. When the oil begins to smoke and the peppers turn dark, remove peppers from pan and discard. □ Brown onion for a few seconds. □ Add cabbage and cook and stir about 1 minute. □ Pour the sauce over cabbage. Cook and stir until the cabbage is tender, about 3 minutes.

- Serve hot.

RADISH SALAD

A light and refreshing way to serve radishes

Preparation time: 20 minutes   Makes 4 servings
Marinating time: 3 hours

SAUCE:
   4 tablespoons vinegar
   4 tablespoons sugar
   2 tablespoons soy sauce
   1 teaspoon sesame oil

   **4 bunches medium-size fresh
   radishes (40-50)**

- Mix sauce ingredients well in a small bowl and set aside.
- Using a small knife, cut off leaves and remove both ends of radishes; wash and dry them. Using the side of a large, heavy knife, gently press the radishes to crush slightly.
- Put radishes in a large bowl. □ Add sauce and mix well. □ Cover and chill for about 3 hours. Stir occasionally.
- Serve cold.

TURNIP SALAD

If you've never tried turnips, this easy dish is a good introduction.

Preparation time: 20 minutes

Makes 4 servings

Marinating time: 20 to 30 minutes

Cooking time: 5 minutes

---

  1 pound turnips (about 2
    large ones)
  1½ teaspoons salt
  1½ tablespoons finely
    chopped green onion
  1 tablespoon sesame oil
  1 tablespoon vegetable oil

PREPARATION:

■ Wash and peel turnips. Cut against the grain into thin slices, then into thin strips. ☐ Put in a bowl and add salt. Mix well with hands, squeezing the salt into the turnips. Set aside for 20 to 30 minutes.

■ Chop onion.

■ Drain juice from turnips by squeezing and kneading the slices. Transfer to serving bowl. Put onions in a small pile on top of the turnips. *Do not mix.*

TO COOK:

■ Heat sesame and vegetable oils together in a small saucepan over high heat until they begin to smoke. ☐ Pour directly over onions, then lightly mix the turnips, onions, and oils together.

■ Serve at room temperature with any meat dish.

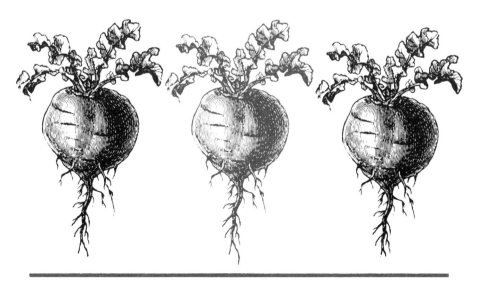

POTATO SALAD— CHINESE STYLE

As a college student in Taiwan, I visited a bakery-sandwich shop where I saw a potato salad sandwich on the menu. As an adventurous eater, I naturally had to sample it. It was delicious—a hot dog bun filled with potato salad and marinated cucumbers. Try this recipe as a sandwhich or with a sandwich. It's also good served with Marinated Baked Chicken.

Preparation time: 40 minutes

Marinating time: 15 minutes

Cooking time: 35 minutes

Makes 6 to 8 servings

4 large potatoes
1 large carrot
4 eggs
2 medium cucumbers

MARINADE:
½ teaspoon salt
2 teaspoons sugar
1 teaspoon vinegar

1 cup cooked cubed ham
½ cup mayonnaise
1 teaspoon salt
¼ teaspoon black pepper

juice of 1 whole lemon
2 tablespoons sunflower seeds (or chopped almonds)

■ Put potatoes and carrots in a large pot, add enough water to cover and bring to a boil over high heat. □ Reduce heat to low and cook 15 to 20 minutes. □ Remove carrot and cook potatoes 10 minutes longer or until just fork-tender.

■ Drain potatoes and let cool. (Refrigerate at least ½ hour.)

■ Hard-boil eggs, peel, and chop. Set aside. □ Cube ham and set aside.

■ Peel and cut cucumbers in half lengthwise. Remove seeds. Cut crosswise into ¼ " slices. □ Add marinade ingredients. Squeeze and rub cucumbers with hands so that the marinade penetrates all slices. Set aside for at least 15 minutes.

■ When ready to assemble salad, remove as much liquid from the cucumbers as possible by squeezing with the hands. Set aside.

■ Peel cooled potatoes and carrots. Cut into small cubes and place in a large bowl. □ Add cubed ham, chopped eggs, and marinated and drained cucumber slices. □ Mix in the mayonnaise, salt, and pepper. □ Add lemon juice. Mix well and chill.

■ Just before serving, garnish chilled salad with sunflower seeds or almonds.

CHICKEN AND CUCUMBER SALAD

This dish is mildly seasoned. If a more pungent taste is desired, add a teaspoon of lemon juice before chilling.

Preparation time: 25 minutes
Marinating time: 30 minutes
Cooking time: 8 minutes

Makes 4 servings

1 whole chicken breast (6-8 ounces)
1 cup water
½ teaspoon salt
2 medium cucumbers

MARINADE:
1 tablespoon chopped onion
1 tablespoon soy sauce
1 tablespoon vinegar
1 tablespoon sugar
1 teaspoon sesame oil
½ teaspoon salt

■ Bone and skin chicken breast.

■ Put water and salt in a small, deep saucepan. □ Add chicken and bring to a boil. Lower heat, cover and cook for about 5 minutes. □ Drain liquid. Let chicken cool.

■ Slice chicken into thin strips and put in serving bowl. □ Peel cucumbers. Cut in half lengthwise and remove seeds. Cut crosswise into thin slices and add to chicken.

■ Mix marinade ingredients and pour over chicken and cucumber slices. □ Mix well. □ Chill 30 minutes. □ Mix well again just before serving.

■ Serve cold.

Note: Do not marinate salad more than 30 minutes before serving — the cucumbers will get too soft. If you want to prepare this dish in advance, combine chicken and cucumber as directed and chill until half an hour before serving. Then pour marinade ingredients over chicken and cucumber mixture and chill again until ready to serve.

RICE & NOODLES

飯或麵

*Even a clever daughter-in-law finds it hard
to cook without rice.*

CHINESE PROVERB

NOTES

99 LBS. NET WEIGHT

WHOLE BEAN
UNCOATED

TABLE RICE

PERFECT BOILED RICE

A recipe for the traditionalist

Preparation time: 5 minutes   Makes 4 servings
Cooking time: 25 minutes

**2 cups pearl rice (round-
grain)
2½ cups water**

PREPARATION:

■ Put rice in deep saucepan. □ Cover with tap water. Stir with hand
or spoon several times. □ Drain and repeat the washing process at
least twice. Drain well.

TO COOK:

■ Add water to washed rice. Cover pan and bring to a quick boil over
high heat. □ Reduce heat to medium-low and cook rice 10 minutes
with cover slightly ajar. (The water should be almost absorbed at
this time.) □ Lower heat and simmer 10 minutes longer with the
cover tightly closed. □ Remove rice from heat and let stand
(covered) until ready to serve.

■ Serve hot.

Note: If you use packaged American-style rice, omit any butter and
salt from the directions. Washing rice removes excess starch. Round-
grain rice is moist, a little sweet, and slightly sticky. Long-grain rice is
tougher and drier.

SHRIMP FRIED RICE

If you like shrimp, this is an especially delicious way to prepare fried rice.

Preparation time: 20 minutes   Makes 4 servings
Cooking time: 30 minutes

¾ **pound raw medium-size
   shrimp**

MARINADE:

½ **teaspoon salt**
1 **teaspoon cooking sherry**
1 **egg**

2 **tablespoons chopped
   green onion**
1 **cup long-grain rice**
2 **cups water**
3 **tablespoons vegetable oil**
½ **cup frozen peas and
   carrots, thawed**
1 **tablespoon soy sauce**
1 **teaspoon sugar**
½ **teaspoon salt**

- Peel and devein shrimp; rinse well and dry with paper towels.
  □ Cut each shrimp in half. □ Thoroughly mix shrimp with marinade ingredients in a small bowl and set aside. □ Chop onion and
  set aside.
- Rinse rice with tap water and drain well. □ Add the water to the
  rice in a medium-size saucepan and bring to a boil over high heat.
  □ Reduce heat to low, cover, and simmer about 20 minutes, until
  all water is absorbed. □ Remove from heat and let stand (covered).
- Heat vegetable oil in wok or large fry pan over medium
  heat. □ Brown onion for a few seconds. □ Add marinated shrimp.
  Stir and cook for about 2 minutes. □ Add peas and carrots. `Stir
  and cook about 30 seconds longer. □ Add cooked rice. Mix
  well. □ Add soy sauce, sugar, and salt. Cook, stirring constantly,
  about 2 more minutes.

- Serve hot.

HAM-AND-EGG FRIED RICE

A popular dish served in Western-style restaurants in Taiwan

Preparation time: 15 minutes

Makes 4 servings

Cooking time: 30 minutes

1 cup long-grain rice
2 cups water
1 cup cooked ham, cubed
2 tablespoons chopped
green onion
3 tablespoons vegetable oil
2 eggs
1 tablespoon soy sauce
¾ teaspoon salt
½ teaspoon sugar

■ Put rice in a medium-size saucepan. □ Rinse several times with tap water. Drain well. □ Add water, cover, and bring to a boil over high heat. □ Reduce heat to low, cover, and simmer 20 minutes, until all liquid is absorbed. □ Remove from heat. Let stand, covered, a few minutes longer.

■ Cube ham. □ Chop onion.

■ Heat vegetable oil in wok or large fry pan over medium heat. □ Beat eggs, and when oil is very hot, pour eggs into pan. □ Scramble lightly, breaking eggs into small pieces. □ Add ham and chopped green onion. Stir well. □ Add cooked rice. Stir well for a few seconds. □ Add soy sauce, salt, and sugar. Stir and cook for about 1 minute longer.

■ Serve hot.

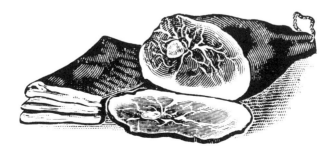

CHICKEN FRIED RICE

This is one of the best ways to make fried rice.

Preparation time: 20 minutes   Makes 4 servings
Cooking time: 35 minutes

1 cup long-grain rice
2 cups water
1 whole chicken breast (6-8
   ounces meat)

MARINADE:

1 teaspoon cornstarch
1 teaspoon soy sauce
½ teaspoon sugar

2 tablespoons chopped
   onion
4 tablespoons vegetable oil
2 eggs
½ cup frozen peas and
   carrots, thawed
1 tablespoon soy sauce
1 teaspoon salt
1 teaspoon sesame oil

■ Rinse rice and drain well. □ Put rice in medium-size saucepan, add water and bring to a boil over high heat. □ Reduce heat, cover, and simmer about 20 minutes, until all liquid is absorbed. □ Remove from heat, keep covered, and let stand for a few minutes longer.

■ Bone and skin chicken; cut it into tiny cubes. □ Combine chicken cubes with marinade ingredients and mix well. Set aside. □ Chop onion.

■ Heat 2 tablespoons vegetable oil in wok or large fry pan over high heat. □ Beat eggs, pour into pan, and scramble lightly, breaking into small pieces. Transfer to a bowl. □ Add remaining vegetable oil to pan. Brown onion for a few seconds over medium heat. □ Add chicken. Cook and stir about 1 minute. □ Add peas and carrots. Cook and stir 30 seconds. □ Add scrambled eggs, stir, and then add cooked rice. Mix well. □ Add soy sauce, salt, and sesame oil. Cook and stir for a few seconds longer. Remove from heat.

■ Serve immediately.

PAN-FRIED SOFT NOODLES

A good all-in-one supper dish

Preparation time: 45 minutes
Cooking time: 7 minutes

Makes 4 servings

½ pound lean beef

MARINADE:

2 teaspoons soy sauce
1 tablespoon cooking sherry
2 teaspoons cornstarch
½ teaspoon sugar

2 tablespoons chopped
   onion
2 large stalks celery
1 medium carrot
8 ounces spaghetti
3 tablespoons vegetable oil
2 eggs
2 tablespoons soy sauce
1 teaspoon sugar
1 teaspoon sesame oil
½ teaspoon salt

PREPARATION:

■ Slice beef against the grain into thin bite-size pieces. □ Mix
marinade ingredients with beef and set aside. □ Cut celery
crosswise into ¼" slices. □ Peel carrot and slice lengthwise in half,
then crosswise in thin slices. Set aside. □ Chop onion and set aside.

TO COOK:

■ Cook spaghetti according to package directions, but do not add salt
to the water. □ Rinse with cold water and drain well.
■ Heat 1 tablespoon of vegetable oil in wok or large fry pan over
medium-high heat. □ Beat eggs and pour into pan. Break apart
and scramble lightly until firm and slightly browned. □ Remove
from pan and set aside. □ Heat the remaining oil. □ Brown onions
for a few seconds. □ Add beef. Cook and stir until the meat changes
color and is cooked through, about 1 minute. □ Add celery and
carrots. Cook and stir about 30 seconds. □ Add scrambled eggs.
Mix well and cook about 30 seconds. □ Add drained spaghetti on
top of other ingredients. □ Add soy sauce, sugar, sesame oil, and
salt. Mix well and cook about 2 minutes longer.

■ Serve hot.

EGG NOODLES WITH MEAT AND VEGETABLE SAUCE

A nutritious family-style dish

Preparation time: 20 minutes

Makes 4 to 6 servings

Cooking time: 6 minutes for meat sauce

10 minutes for noodles

SAUCE:

2 tablespoons ketchup
2 tablespoons soy sauce
1 teaspoon sugar
1 teaspoon salt
2 teaspoons sesame oil
¼ teaspoon black pepper
¾ cup water

½ cup chopped fresh mushrooms
½ medium green pepper
3 tablespoons chopped onion
1 tablespoon vegetable oil
1 pound lean ground beef
½ cup frozen peas and carrots, thawed
2 tablespoons cornstarch dissolved in 4 tablespoons water
1½ quarts water
1 tablespoon salt
1 package (8 ounces) wide egg noodles

PREPARATION:

- Mix sauce ingredients in a small bowl and set aside.
- Chop mushrooms. □ Remove stem and seeds from green pepper. Cut pepper into ¼″ pieces. □ Chop onion.

TO COOK:

- Heat vegetable oil in a wok or large fry pan over high heat. □ Brown ground beef for about 2 minutes, stirring constantly. □ Add chopped onion, peas and carrots, mushrooms, and green peppers. Stir and cook 1 minute. □ Add sauce mixture. Bring to boil over high heat. □ Stir and cook about 2 minutes. □ Add dissolved cornstarch to the center of the pan. Stir sauce about 30 seconds until it has thickened slightly. □ Remove from heat. Cover and set aside.
- Put water and salt in a large pot. Bring to boil over high heat. □ Add egg noodles. Stir well and cook uncovered 5 minutes. Stir occasionally. (Be careful not to overcook.)
- Drain noodles well. □ Put on a large plate and spoon meat sauce evenly over the hot noodles. (The sauce can also be mixed with the noodles if you prefer.)
- Serve immediately.

COLD SPICY NOODLES

Served cold, these noodles go well with any meat entrée and are especially good as a summertime dish or for a picnic.

Preparation time: 20 minutes   Makes 4 to 6 servings
Cooking time: 20 minutes

8 ounces thin spaghetti
5 cups water
2½ teaspoons salt
1 medium cucumber

SAUCE:

1 dried red chili pepper
1 clove garlic
2 tablespoons finely
chopped green onion
2 tablespoons soy sauce
2 teaspoons sesame oil
2 teaspoons vinegar
1 tablespoon water
½ teaspoon sugar

■ Put water and salt in a medium-size saucepan and bring to a boil over high heat. ☐ Break spaghetti in half. Add to boiling water and stir. Cook 15 minutes, stirring occasionally.

■ Meanwhile, peel cucumber and cut in half lengthwise. Scoop out seeds with a spoon. Cut into 2″ chunks. Cut chunks lengthwise into very thin slivers. ☐ Put in a bowl and set aside.

■ Remove pot of spaghetti from heat. Drain spaghetti and rinse with cold water. *Drain well.* ☐ Put in a large bowl and set aside.

■ Break chili pepper in pieces. ☐ Peel and lightly crush garlic. ☐ Chop onion. ☐ Mix sauce ingredients in a small saucepan. ☐ Bring to boil over high heat and boil for a few seconds. Remove from heat. Discard garlic and red pepper.

■ Pour sauce over cooled spaghetti. Mix well. ☐ Transfer to a serving plate. ☐ Sprinkle cucumber slivers on top of spaghetti.

■ Serve at room temperature, or refrigerate and serve cold.

PAN-FRIED MACARONI

When I was a teenager in Taiwan, I saw a package of macaroni in a Western shop; naturally I took it home and experimented with it. After many tries, I finally discovered that it was necessary to boil the macaroni before combining it with the other ingredients!

Preparation time: 20 minutes   Makes 4 to 6 servings
Cooking time: 5 minutes

½ **pound lean pork**

MARINADE:

1 tablespoon soy sauce
2 teaspoons cornstarch
½ teaspoon sugar

2 tablespoons chopped
   onion
2 cups coarsely shredded
   cabbage
1 quart water
2 teaspoons salt
8 ounces small macaroni
2 tablespoons vegetable oil
1 tablespoon soy sauce
2 tablespoons ketchup
1 teaspoon sugar

PREPARATION:

■ Cut pork against the grain into thin strips. □ Mix well with marinade ingredients and set aside.
■ Shred cabbage. □ Chop onion.

TO COOK:

■ Bring water and salt to boil. □ Add macaroni and cook 6 minutes. □ Drain and rinse with cold water. Set aside.
■ Heat vegetable oil in wok or large fry pan over high heat. □ Brown onion for a few seconds. □ Add marinated pork. Cook and stir about 1 minute. □ Add cabbage. Cook and stir about 1 minute longer. □ Add boiled macaroni. Mix well. □ Add soy sauce, ketchup and sugar. Stir and cook about 2 minutes longer.

■ Serve hot. (Serves four as main dish or six as side dish.)

EGGGS & MIS-CELLANEOUS

蛋和其它

New dishes beget new appetites.

NOTES

EGGS AND TOMATOES

Serve for brunch or luncheon with steamed or boiled rice. Add other dishes such as Stir-Fry Shrimp with Peas and/or Chicken Fried Rice for a larger meal.

Preparation time: 15 minutes   Makes 4 servings
Cooking time: 5 minutes

2 medium tomatoes
2 tablespoons chopped
  green onion
6 eggs
4 tablespoons vegetable oil
1½ tablespoons soy sauce
1 teaspoon sugar
1 teaspoon salt

PREPARATION:

■ Cut tomatoes in quarters and then in bite-size pieces. □ Chop onion.

■ Beat eggs with chopped onion.

TO COOK:

■ Heat vegetable oil in wok or fry pan over high heat. □ When the oil is very hot, pour in the egg mixture. Stir and cook over high heat until the eggs are firm and slightly dry. □ Add tomatoes. Stir well and cook about 1 minute. □ Add soy sauce, sugar, and salt. Cook and stir about 1 minute longer.

■ Serve hot.

EGGS AND CRABMEAT

An easy brunch dish

Preparation time: 10 minutes   Makes 4 servings
Cooking time: 5 minutes

SAUCE:

2 tablespoons water
1 tablespoon soy sauce
2 teaspoons cooking sherry
1 teaspoon salt
½ teaspoon sugar

2 tablespoons chopped
** green onion**
5 eggs
4 tablespoons vegetable oil
6 ounces fresh cooked
** crabmeat**

PREPARATION:

- Mix sauce ingredients in a small bowl and set aside.
- Chop onion.
- Beat eggs.

TO COOK:

- Heat vegetable oil in wok or fry pan over high heat. □ Brown onions for a few seconds. □ Add beaten eggs. Cook and stir until eggs are almost firm. □ Add crabmeat and stir for a few seconds. □ Add sauce and cook and stir about 30 seconds longer.

- Serve immediately.

Note: If fresh crab is not available, use canned crab and reduce salt to ½ teaspoon.

SCRAMBLED EGGS WITH BEEF

A good brunch dish for four people

Preparation time: 25 minutes
Cooking time: 5 minutes

Makes 4 servings

½ pound lean beef

MARINADE:

1 tablespoon soy sauce
1 tablespoon cooking sherry
2 teaspoons cornstarch
½ teaspoon sugar
¼ teaspoon salt
⅛ teaspoon ginger powder

1 tablespoon finely chopped
green onion
6 eggs
½ teaspoon salt
4 tablespoons vegetable oil

PREPARATION:

- Cut beef against the grain into thin 1″ pieces.
- Thoroughly mix sliced beef with marinade ingredients in a small bowl and set aside.
- Chop onion.
- In a large bowl, beat eggs with the onion and salt. Set aside.

TO COOK:

- Heat 2 tablespoons vegetable oil in wok or large fry pan over high heat. □ When the oil is hot, add marinated beef. Stir and cook about 1 minute. □ When the beef changes color and is almost cooked through, immediately transfer beef to beaten egg mixture. Mix well. □ Wipe the fry pan with a paper towel. Return to high heat. □ Add remaining vegetable oil. □ When the oil is hot, add beef and egg mixture. Stir gently. Cook until eggs are firm but not dry, about 1 minute. □ Remove from heat.

- Serve immediately.

STEAMED EGG-AND-MEAT PUDDING

This is a family meal eaten quite often in China. Mothers like to serve it to children because it is tasty and nutritious as well as easy to prepare.

Preparation time: 20 minutes

Cooking time: 25 minutes

Makes 4 servings

6 eggs
6 tablespoons water
½ teaspoon salt
½ pound lean ground pork

MARINADE:

**2 tablespoons finely
chopped green onion**
2 tablespoons water
1 tablespoon soy sauce
1 teaspoon cooking sherry
1 teaspoon sugar
½ teaspoon salt
1 teaspoon sesame oil

1 teaspoon sesame oil
2 cups water

PREPARATION:

- Using a fork, beat eggs with water and salt in a large bowl for at least 1 minute. Set aside.

- Chop onion. □ Thoroughly mix marinade ingredients with pork in a small bowl. Use a fork and be sure to mix very well. □ Add marinated pork to eggs and mix very well. Make sure the pork is broken up and not lumpy.

- Put sesame oil in a clean 7"-diameter heat-proof bowl. Tilt bowl and, using index finger, coat bowl with oil. □ Pour egg and pork mixture into oiled bowl. Set aside.

TO COOK:

- Put water in a 10" pot. □ Set bowl containing the egg and meat mixture in water. Cover pot and steam over high heat for about 25 minutes. □ Test firmness with fork. □ When slightly firm, remove from heat.

- To serve, spoon over hot, boiled rice.

EGG PIE WITH SPICY MEAT SAUCE

An unusual and easy way to make a simple egg dish more interesting and tastier

Preparation time: 25 minutes
Cooking time: 16 minutes

Makes 8 servings

6 eggs
1 tablespoon cornstarch
  dissolved in 2 tablespoons
  water
½ teaspoon salt
1 teaspoon vegetable oil

SAUCE:
1 tablespoon soy sauce
1 teaspoon cornstarch
1 teaspoon sugar
4 tablespoons water
2 teaspoons vinegar
1 tablespoon cooking sherry
¼ teaspoon ginger powder
¼ teaspoon salt

2 cloves garlic
1 dried red chili pepper
2 tablespoons finely
  chopped green onion

2 tablespoons vegetable oil
½ pound lean ground beef

PREPARATION:

■ Using a fork, beat eggs in a large bowl with dissolved cornstarch, salt and vegetable oil until foamy. Set aside.

■ Thoroughly mix sauce ingredients in a small bowl and set aside.

■ Peel garlic and chop fine. □ Break chili pepper into small pieces. □ Chop onion.

TO COOK:

■ Heat vegetable oil in a 10″ fry pan over medium-high heat. □ When the oil is very hot, add beaten egg mixture. Reduce heat to low, cover, and slowly cook 8 to 10 minutes. □ When the eggs are almost firm, raise heat to medium. Turn egg pie over. Brown other side for about 30 seconds. □ Leaving the oil in the pan, transfer egg pie to a serving plate and set aside or keep warm in oven.

■ Add onion, garlic and dried red chili pepper to the pan. Brown for a few seconds. □ Add ground beef. Stir constantly over medium heat and cook about 2 minutes.

■ Stir sauce well. □ Add to beef mixture in pan. Cook and stir for about 1 minute longer. □ Remove from heat. Spoon sauce evenly over egg pie.

■ Cut in eight wedges with a sharp knife and serve hot.

CHICKEN AND VEGETABLE EGG PIE

A nutritious and attractive dish that can be served for any meal of the day

Preparation time: 25 minutes

Cooking time: 30 minutes

Makes 4 servings

6 ounces raw chicken

MARINADE:

1 teaspoon soy sauce
1 teaspoon cooking sherry
1 teaspoon cornstarch
½ teaspoon sugar

2 tablespoons chopped onion
½ cup cooked cubed ham
4 tablespoons vegetable oil
½ cup frozen peas and carrots, thawed

2 teaspoons chopped water chestnuts (if desired)
½ teaspoon salt
½ teaspoon sesame oil
6 eggs
½ teaspoon salt

PREPARATION:

■ Bone and skin chicken. Cut in strips and then into small cubes. □ Mix marinade ingredients with chicken in a small bowl. Set aside.

■ Chop onion. □ Cube ham.

TO COOK:

■ Preheat oven to low.

■ Heat 2 tablespoons vegetable oil in fry pan over medium-high heat. □ Brown onions for a few seconds. □ Add marinated chicken. Cook and stir until the chicken changes color, about 1 minute. □ Add peas and carrots, water chestnuts, and ham. Cook and stir about 30 seconds. □ Add salt and sesame oil and stir 30 seconds longer. □ Transfer filling to a bowl.

■ Heat 1 tablespoon vegetable oil in 10″ fry pan over medium-high heat. □ Beat eggs with salt. When the oil is hot, pour in a little less than half of the beaten egg mixture. Do not stir. Tipping pan to set surface, cook egg pancake until almost firm. □ Carefully transfer to a plate, browned side down. Keep warm in oven. □ Heat the remaining vegetable oil in the pan over medium-high heat. □ When the oil is hot, pour in the remaining egg mixture. Tip pan as before, cooking until the bottom of the egg pancake is firm and the top is slightly soft. □ Lower heat. Spread filling over pancake. Cook about 30 seconds. □ Remove first pancake from oven and put on top of filling, browned side up. Cook a few seconds longer. □ Carefully transfer filled pie to a serving plate by pushing with a large spatula.

■ Using a sharp knife, cut in quarters and serve immediately.

SAUTÉED CHICKEN LIVERS

The sauce is what makes this dish so delicious.

Preparation time: 20 minutes   Makes 4 servings
Cooking time: 5 minutes

1½ pounds chicken livers
1 cup green onion pieces

SAUCE:
2½ tablespoons soy sauce
1 tablespoon water
1½ tablespoons cooking sherry
1 teaspoon sugar
¼ teaspoon salt
2 teaspoons cornstarch
⅛ teaspoon black pepper
1 teaspoon sesame oil

3 tablespoons vegetable oil

PREPARATION:

■ Rinse chicken livers and pat dry with paper towels. □ Cut livers into 1½" pieces. □ Cut green onion in 1½" pieces.
■ Mix sauce ingredients in a small bowl and set aside.

TO COOK:

■ Heat vegetable oil in wok or large fry pan over medium-high heat. □ Brown onions for a few seconds. □ Add livers. Cook and stir about 2 minutes. (The livers should be just slightly pink.) □ Stir sauce well and pour into the pan. □ Mix sauce with livers and cook and stir about 1 minute longer.

■ Serve immediately.

SPICY CALVES' LIVER

Liver should be served tender and juicy, never overcooked or dried out.

Preparation time: 25 minutes   Makes 4 servings
Cooking time: 5 minutes

SAUCE:
   1 tablespoon soy sauce
   1 teaspoon sugar
   ½ teaspoon salt
   1 teaspoon cornstarch
   1 tablespoon water
   ½ teaspoon sesame oil

   1 pound calves' liver
   3 tablespoons vegetable oil
      dried red chili peppers (2
      or 3)
   ½ cup thinly sliced onion
   3 cloves garlic

PREPARATION:
- Mix sauce ingredients in a small bowl and set aside.
- Slice liver into strips 1½″ by ¼″. □ Cut onion into thin slices. □ Peel and crush garlic.

TO COOK:
- Heat vegetable oil in large fry pan over high heat. □ Add chili peppers. Brown for a few seconds. When the peppers turn dark, discard. □ Add sliced onions and garlic cloves and brown for a few seconds. (If desired, discard garlic.) □ Add liver. Stir constantly until the liver changes color, about 2 minutes. □ Add sauce ingredients and cook and stir about 45 seconds longer.

- Serve immediately.

VEAL STEW

This stew is cooked at a higher temperature than beef stew because veal cooks faster than beef, and the vegetables must cook quickly over high heat to remain crisp yet tender.

Preparation time: 25 minutes
Cooking time: 1 hour

Makes 4 to 6 servings

½ **medium onion**
2 **pounds veal for stew**
3 **tablespoons vegetable oil**
2½ **cups water**
3 **tablespoons soy sauce**
2 **tablespoons cooking sherry**
2 **teaspoons sugar**
½ **teaspoon black pepper**
½ **teaspoon ginger powder**
2 **medium carrots**
2 **large stalks celery**
½ **pound fresh string beans**
1 **teaspoon salt**

- Chop onion. □ Cut veal into 2″ chunks.
- Heat vegetable oil in a large, deep saucepan over high heat. □ Brown onion for a few seconds. □ Add veal. Stir and brown for about 1 minute. □ Add 1 cup of the water and bring to a boil. □ Add soy sauce, sherry, sugar, pepper, and ginger powder. Stir well. □ Cover and lower heat to medium. Cook 30 minutes, stirring occasionally. (The liquid should be almost absorbed.)
- Meanwhile peel carrots and cut into 1″ chunks. □ Cut celery into 1″ chunks. □ Remove ends from string beans and cut or break into 1″ pieces.
- Add the remaining water to the veal; add carrots, celery, beans, and salt. Stir well. □ Cover and cook for about 25 minutes, stirring occasionally. The veal and vegetables should be tender but not mushy. □ Remove from heat.
- Serve hot.

CHINESE-STYLE PANCAKES

These pancakes are usually filled with Mu Shu Pork, but you can use your imagination and experiment with other fillings.

Preparation time: 50 minutes
Cooking time: 12 minutes

Makes 8 pancakes

2 cups all-purpose flour
¾ cup boiling water
1 tablespoon vegetable oil
in a small dish

PREPARATION:

- Put flour in a large bowl. □ Add the boiling water. Mix with fork until slightly cooled. □ Knead for about 1 minute. The dough may be a little lumpy. □ Form the dough into a rope and divide into eight equal pieces. Roll each piece into a ball and then flatten with the palm of the hand.
- Take two pieces, one in each hand. Dip one side of each in the small dish containing the oil. Press oiled sides together and flatten to make a 3½" circle (like a filled cookie without the filling.) □ Roll into a thin circle approximately 7" in diameter. □ Repeat, making three more pairs of two pancakes each.

TO COOK:

- Preheat oven to low.
- Warm a 10" ungreased fry pan over medium-low heat. □ Place one pancake (two layers) in the pan. Lower heat slightly and cook about 45 seconds on each side. Then cook the first side again for about 15 seconds. □ Remove from pan and peel the layers apart carefully. Immediately place in a covered casserole, laying the pancakes as flat as possible. □ Keep the covered dish in warm oven until ready to serve. (The pancakes should always be warm, soft, and moist.)
- To serve, put about 3 tablespoons of desired filling in the center of the warm pancake. □ Fold the sides over and roll the pancake. The pancakes are then picked up and eaten with the hands.

Note: The pancakes can be prepared in advance. Peel the layers and put in a covered casserole to cool. The dish must be covered to retain moisture. When cool, carefully place the pancakes in a plastic bag and seal tightly. Freeze. □ When ready to serve, defrost pancakes in the bag. Then wrap tightly in foil and heat in oven at 300° F. for a few minutes.

SWEETS & DESSERTS

點心

It is difficult to satisfy one's appetite
by painting pictures of cakes.

CHINESE PROVERB

NOTES

ALMOND COOKIES

This is one of the most popular American-Chinese desserts.

Preparation time: 45 minutes
Cooking time: 14 minutes

Makes 2 dozen cookies

> **2 eggs**
> **6 tablespoons sugar**
> **2½ cups flour**
> **½ teaspoon baking soda**
> **½ cup margarine, softened but not melted**
> **1 tablespoon almond extract**
> **24 almonds (or almond halves)**
> **1 beaten egg**

PREPARATION:

- Preheat oven to 375 °F.
- Beat the eggs with sugar. □ Add flour, baking soda, margarine and almond extract. Mix well with a fork. □ Knead dough until smooth.
- Divide dough into two equal parts. Form into two long ropes. □ Divide each rope into four equal parts. □ Divide each part into three pieces. □ Roll each piece into a ball (twenty-four total).
- Using hands, flatten each ball into a 3″ circle and place on an ungreased cookie sheet. □ Press an almond or almond half in the center of each and brush tops of cookies with beaten egg.

TO COOK:

- Bake 14 minutes, until light brown. □ Remove cookies from cookie sheet and let cool thoroughly. □ Store in a tightly closed container.

CRISPY TEA COOKIES

A good recipe for beginning cooks, these are nice to serve as a light dessert with tea.

Preparation time: 1 hour
Cooking time: 20 minutes

Makes about 4 dozen cookies

2 large eggs
4 tablespoons sugar
1 tablespoon water
2 cups all-purpose flour
2 tablespoons powdered
   sugar
3 cups vegetable oil (approx.)

PREPARATION:

- Beat eggs with sugar and water in a large bowl. □ Add flour. Mix with hands and knead until smooth, soft and workable.
- Divide dough into four equal parts. On a floured board, flatten and roll each part into a long, neat rectangle (about 9″ by 4″), ⅛″ thick. Cut each rectangle in half. Put one piece of dough on top of the other. Cut through the two pieces to make thin strips, 4″ by ¼″. You will cut seventeen times, making thirty-six strips (eighteen double strips).
- Press the top ends of three strips together and braid tightly. Press bottom ends together. Repeat until all strips are used. Set aside. Repeat entire process with remaining dough (three more double rectangle halves to cut).

TO COOK:

- Heat vegetable oil in a wok or large fry pan over medium-high heat. □ When the oil is hot, drop in one braid at a time, keeping each as straight as possible. Fry 1 to 2 dozen braids at a time, depending on size of pan. □ Turn braids once while frying so that each will brown evenly. Frying time will be about 5 minutes for each batch. □ Remove from pan onto a cookie sheet. □ Let cool slightly and sprinkle with powdered sugar.

PEANUT BUTTER COOKIES

A favorite of our children, these cookies are neither too sweet nor too rich.

Preparation time: 45 minutes
Cooking time: 8 minutes

Makes 32 cookies

3 tablespoons margarine, softened but not melted
3 tablespoons sesame seeds
3 tablespoons smooth peanut butter
3 tablespoons sugar
1 egg
½ teaspoon baking soda
1 cup flour

PREPARATION:

- Preheat oven to 400°F.
- In a large bowl, thoroughly mix margarine, sesame seeds, peanut butter, sugar, and egg with a wooden spoon until the mixture resembles a soft paste. □ Add baking soda and flour. Mix well and knead with hands until smooth and soft.
- Divide dough in half, then in quarters. □ With hands, roll each piece into a long rope. □ Divide each rope into eight pieces (thirty-two total). □ Using palms of hands, roll each piece into a ball. □ Flatten each to a 1½″ to 2″ circle.

TO COOK:

- Place on an ungreased cookie sheet on the middle rack of oven. Bake about 8 minutes until light brown. □ Remove from oven immediately. (Do not overbake—cookies burn very easily.) Remove cookies from cookie sheet and let cool.

CRUSHED PEANUT AND SESAME PASTRIES

These are unique in flavor—rich, yet light and easy to make.

Preparation time: 45 minutes   Makes 12 pastries
Cooking time: 15 minutes

¼ **cup dry roasted peanuts**
1½ **tablespoons vegetable oil**
2 **tablespoons sesame
    seeds**
3 **tablespoons sugar**
6 **frozen patty shells, thawed
    powdered sugar**

■ Finely chop peanuts in a blender or food processor, or put them in the plastic bag and crush with a rolling pin.
■ Heat vegetable oil in wok or small fry pan over medium heat. □ When the oil is warm, add crushed peanuts, sesame seeds, and sugar. Stir and brown lightly (about 30 seconds to 1 minute). □ Remove from heat and let cool.
■ Preheat oven to 400°F.
■ Cut each patty shell in half. □ Roll each half into a ball and flatten with palm of hand. Roll out each flattened shell-half into a 4″ circle. □ Hold rolled-out circle in palm of hand. With other hand, put 1 tablespoon filling in center of circle. Fold dough over and pinch *tightly* to seal. (The dough must be sealed tightly or the filling will leak during baking.)
■ Bake on an ungreased cookie sheet in oven for 15 minutes or until light brown and puffy.

■ Dust with powdered sugar. Serve hot or warm.

EGG CUSTARD TART

A famous dessert served at Cantonese brunches

Preparation time: 45 minutes   Makes 12 tarts
Cooking time: 50 minutes

PASTRY:

1½ cups all-purpose flour
6 tablespoons margarine,
   softened but not melted
3 tablespoons water
¾ teaspoon baking powder

FILLING:

2 eggs
6 tablespoons sugar
½ cup water

- Mix flour with margarine, water, and baking powder. □ Knead until smooth. □ Divide dough into four equal parts. Then divide each part into thirds, roll each piece into a ball, making twelve balls of dough.
- Preheat oven to 250°F.
- Flatten one ball slightly. Roll with a rolling pin into a 4″ circle. □ Gently press into an ungreased muffin tin. □ Repeat with remaining dough.
- Bake on next-to-lowest rack in oven for 20 minutes.
- While the pastry shells are baking, prepare filling. □ In a small bowl, mix eggs, sugar and water. Beat with a fork until the sugar dissolves. □ Pour the mixture through a strainer into another bowl. (This makes the filling smoother.)
- Remove muffin tin from oven. Fill pastry-lined tins three-quarters full with strained filling. □ Return to oven and bake 25 to 30 minutes until the tops are shiny and just slightly firm. □ Cool slightly and remove tarts from tin.

- Serve warm.

ALMOND FRUIT GELATIN

In Taiwan, in addition to the fruit cocktail, we also used canned lichee nuts, canned loquats or canned mandarin oranges to prepare this light, refreshing dessert.

Preparation time: 20 minutes

Cooking time: 5 minutes

Chilling time: 2 hours

Makes 4 servings

1 package unflavored gelatin
¾ cup water
4 tablespoons sugar
1 cup cold milk
1½ teaspoons almond extract
1 can (1 pound 1 ounce) fruit cocktail, undrained canned lichee nuts and loquats or mandarin oranges (if desired)

■ Put water in a small saucepan and sprinkle gelatin over the water. □ Place saucepan over low heat, add 3 tablespoons of the sugar and stir until the gelatin and sugar are dissolved (about 3 minutes). □ Remove from heat and let cool. □ Add milk and almond extract. Mix well.

■ Pour mixture to a depth of 1″ into one or two pans, depending upon size of pan. □ Chill until very firm, at least 2 hours.

■ When gelatin is firm, pour fruit cocktail and nuts and other fruits, if desired, into a large serving bowl. □ Add ½ can water and the remaining sugar. Stir well.

■ Rinse bottom of gelatin pan with warm water to loosen gelatin. □ Using a small knife, cut gelatin into cubes. □ With a spatula, remove cubes from pan and add to the bowl of fruit cocktail. Gently stir to mix well and return to refrigerator.

■ Serve chilled.

INDEX

Table of Measures

DRY METRIC CONVERSION

½ teaspoon	2½ grams
1 teaspoon	5 grams
1 tablespoon	14 grams
1 ounce	28 grams
4 ounces (¼ pound)	113 grams
8 ounces (½ pound)	226 grams
16 ounces (1 pound)	500 grams

LIQUID* METRIC CONVERSIONS

1 teaspoon	5 milliliters
1 tablespoon (3 teaspoons)	15 milliliters
1 ounce (2 tablespoons)	30 milliliters
¼ cup	60 milliliters
⅓ cup	75 milliliters
½ cup (4 ounces)	125 milliliters
1 cup (8 ounces)	250 milliliters (¼ liter)
2 cups (1 pint)	500 milliliters (½ liter)
4 cups (1 quart)	1000 milliliters (1 liter)

*metric equivalents slightly rounded

NOTES